Canadian Living's Best
Appetizers
Made Easy

BY

Elizabeth Baird

AND

The Food Writers of Canadian Living® Magazine
and The Canadian Living Test Kitchen

A MADISON PRESS BOOK
PRODUCED FOR
BALLANTINE BOOKS AND CANADIAN LIVING

Ballantine Books
A Division of
Random House of
Canada Limited
2775 Matheson Blvd East
Mississauga, Ontario
Canada
L4W 4P7

Canadian Living
Telemedia
Communications Inc.
25 Sheppard Avenue West
Suite 100
North York, Ontario
Canada
M2N 6S7

Canadian Cataloguing in Publication Data

Baird, Elizabeth
Appetizers made easy

(Canadian Living's Best)
"Produced for Ballantine Books and Canadian Living."
Includes index.
ISBN 0-345-39871-8

1. Appetizers. I. Title. II. Series.

TX740.B34 1998   641.8'12   C98-931336-0

EDITORIAL DIRECTOR: Hugh Brewster

PROJECT EDITOR: Wanda Nowakowska

EDITORIAL ASSISTANCE: Beverley Renahan, Rosemary Hillary

PRODUCTION DIRECTOR: Susan Barrable

PRODUCTION COORDINATOR: Donna Chong

BOOK DESIGN AND LAYOUT: Gordon Sibley Design Inc.

COLOR SEPARATION: Colour Technologies

PRINTING AND BINDING: Imprimeries Transcontinental Inc.

CANADIAN LIVING ADVISORY BOARD: Elizabeth Baird, Bonnie Baker Cowan,
Anna Hobbs, Caren King

CANADIAN LIVING'S BEST APPETIZERS MADE EASY
was produced by Madison Press Books
which is under the direction of Albert E. Cummings

Madison Press Books
40 Madison Avenue
Toronto, Ontario, Canada
M5R 2S1

Printed in Canada

Contents

Crostini con Funghi (p. 12)

Brie with Cranberry Chutney (p. 31)

For list of appetizers on platter, see p. 74.

On front cover (clockwise from center): Thai Crab Salad Phyllo Cup (p. 57), Cheesy Crostini (p. 21), stuffed Belgian endive (p. 11)

Introduction

Appetizers offer a delicious welcome to friends and family, whatever the entertaining occasion. More than any other kind of food, they capture the spirit of hospitality we extend whenever we invite people to our homes. So it's important that any collection of appetizer recipes should suit the many different occasions on which we entertain, both at home and within our communities.

And that's exactly what you'll find in this invaluable new entertaining cookbook from *Canadian Living. Appetizers Made Easy* features over 100 of our very best munchable morsels for every entertaining occasion — from summery tomato-topped bruschetta and toast cups brimming with shrimp to elegant pâtés and terrines, quick dips and savory spreads, freeze-ahead phyllo tidbits and intriguing satays and kabobs. In short, everything you need to entertain in style — whether you're tuning in to a video party, hosting a momentous reception, starting a dinner party or opening your house for an afternoon or evening with friends and neighbors.

This collection of welcome-to-our-house starters features recipes from Canada's finest food writers, especially the ones who have contributed over the years to *Canadian Living* cookbooks — Bonnie Stern, Anne Lindsay, Rose Murray, Daphna Rabinovitch, Marg Fraser and Carol Ferguson. The Canadian Living Test Kitchen has also added considerably to this special cookbook, not only with delicious recipes but also with the "tested till perfect" stamp of approval that cooks everywhere have learned to trust.

So, whether you call them hors d'oeuvres, canapés, appetizers, starters or snacks, welcome to the world of happy nibbling in the company of the people you love.

Elizabeth Baird

Spicy Bean Dip (p. 44)

Nibbles on Bread

Some of the very best appetizer bites come on bread —
from dainty canapés and toast cups to funky bruschetta
and crowd-pleasing mini pita pockets.

Smoked Salmon Cornucopias ▶

Cones of pink salmon, a creamy spread and cocktail-size squares of dark rye come together for a truly pleasing sight and bite. Guests will be impressed — and so will you, when you see how quick these are to make.

Per piece: about
- 52 calories
- 2 g fat
- 3 g protein
- 6 g carbohydrate

1/4 cup	minced fresh dill	50 mL
1 tbsp	vegetable oil	15 mL
1 tbsp	grainy Dijon mustard	15 mL
2 tsp	vinegar	10 mL
1/4 tsp	each dry mustard and granulated sugar	1 mL
4 oz	light cream cheese, softened	125 g
1	pkg (250 g) cocktail pumpernickel bread	1
5 oz	thinly sliced smoked salmon	150 g
48	capers	48
24	fresh dill sprigs	24

● In small bowl, mix together dill, oil, Dijon mustard, vinegar, dry mustard and sugar; mix in cream cheese until blended. *(Spread can be refrigerated in airtight container for up to 2 days.)*

● Spread 1 tsp (5 mL) cheese mixture onto each of 24 slices of cocktail bread. Shape salmon pieces into cones about same width as bread square; place on cheese, seam side down. Place 2 capers and 1 dill sprig in each cone. Makes 24 pieces.

Onion Cheese Bites ▶

This is the ultimate drop-in appetizer and an all-ages favorite. Keep all the ingredients on hand, especially over holiday weekends and the party season.

Per piece: about
- 89 calories
- 4 g fat
- 3 g protein
- 10 g carbohydrate

12	diagonal slices (3/4-inch/2 cm thick) baguette (French stick)	12
1/2 cup	freshly grated Parmesan or Romano cheese	125 mL
1/3 cup	chopped green onion	75 mL
1/3 cup	light mayonnaise	75 mL
1 tbsp	finely chopped sweet red pepper	15 mL
	Pepper	

● Arrange bread slices on baking sheet; broil for 1 to 2 minutes or just until lightly browned.

● In small bowl, stir together cheese, onion, mayonnaise and red pepper. *(Cheese mixture can be refrigerated in airtight container for up to 24 hours.)* Turn toasts over. Spread heaping 1 tsp (5 mL) on untoasted side of slices; sprinkle with pepper to taste. Broil 6 inches (15 cm) from heat, watching closely, for 1 to 2 minutes or until browned and bubbly. Makes 12 pieces.

*(Silver plate) Smoked Salmon Cornucopias, Onion Cheese Bites;
(round plate) Shrimp Croustades, Chèvre and Roasted Pepper Bruschetta (p. 13)*

Scallop and Avocado Bruschetta ▶

Coriander, also known as cilantro, is the most widely used herb in the world. Enjoy it in this luxurious Latin-style topping.

Per serving: about
• 163 calories   • 7 g protein
• 10 g fat   • 12 g carbohydrate

4	large scallops (about 4 oz/125 g)	4
1 tbsp	extra virgin olive oil	15 mL
1-1/2 tsp	chopped fresh coriander	7 mL
Pinch	pepper	Pinch
Half	avocado, peeled	Half
2 tsp	lime juice	10 mL
Pinch	salt	Pinch
4	slices baguette (French stick), grilled	4
1	plum tomato, sliced	1

● Cut scallops in half horizontally. In small bowl, stir together oil, coriander and half of the pepper; add scallops, turning to coat. Place on greased grill over medium-high heat; close lid and cook, turning once, for 3 minutes or just until slightly firm and opaque. Let cool slightly.

● In bowl, coarsely mash together avocado, lime juice, salt and remaining pepper; spread over grilled bread. Top with tomato and scallop slices. Makes 4 servings.

Peppery Bruschetta ▶

Sweet peppers intertwine in a colorful toss atop grilled Italian bread.

Per serving: about
• 237 calories   • 4 g protein
• 14 g fat   • 25 g carbohydrate

1	each large sweet red, yellow and green pepper	1
3 tbsp	extra virgin olive oil	50 mL
1 tbsp	chopped fresh basil	15 mL
1	clove garlic, minced	1
1 tsp	balsamic or red wine vinegar	5 mL
Pinch	each salt and pepper	Pinch
4	large slices Italian bread, grilled	4

● Place red, yellow and green peppers on greased grill over medium-high heat; close lid and cook, turning four times, for about 25 minutes or until charred. Let cool. Peel, core and seed; cut into thin strips.

● In bowl, stir together peppers, oil, basil, garlic, vinegar, salt and pepper; cover and let stand for at least 30 minutes or for up to 2 hours. Spoon onto grilled bread. Makes 4 servings.

Grilled Onion and Goat Cheese Bruschetta ▶

Grilling onions tames their harshness and makes this appetizer perfectly pleasing for polite company.

Per serving: about
• 147 calories   • 7 g protein
• 10 g fat   • 11 g carbohydrate

1	small red onion	1
1 tbsp	extra virgin olive oil	15 mL
Pinch	each salt and pepper	Pinch
3 tbsp	cream goat cheese (chèvre), softened	50 mL
1 tbsp	pesto	15 mL
4	slices baguette (French stick), grilled	4

● Cut onion into 1/4-inch (5 mm) thick slices. Place on greased grill over medium-high heat. Brush with 2 tsp (10 mL) of the oil; sprinkle with salt and pepper. Close lid and cook, turning once and brushing with remaining oil, for about 10 minutes or until tender but slices still hold together. Let cool slightly.

● Meanwhile, in small bowl, stir goat cheese with pesto; spread over grilled bread. Top with onion. Makes 4 servings.

(Clockwise from top) Tomato Arugula Bruschetta, Peppery Bruschetta, Grilled Onion and Goat Cheese Bruschetta, Scallop and Avocado Bruschetta

Tomato Arugula Bruschetta ▲

1-1/2 cups	chopped yellow or red tomatoes	375 mL	4	large slices Italian bread, grilled	4
1 tbsp	chopped fresh oregano	15 mL			
1 tbsp	extra virgin olive oil	15 mL			
1	clove garlic, minced	1			
Pinch	each salt and pepper	Pinch			
1/2 cup	small arugula leaves	125 mL			

● In bowl, gently toss together tomatoes, oregano, oil, garlic, salt and pepper; cover and let stand for 30 minutes. Add arugula; toss to combine. Spoon onto grilled bread, spreading evenly. Makes 4 servings.

Funky arugula teams up with summer-ripe tomatoes for a refreshing new take on an entertaining favorite.

Per serving: about
- 160 calories
- 7 g fat
- 4 g protein
- 21 g carbohydrate

Garlic Cheese Toasts ▶

Full of flavor and crunch, these cheesy mouthfuls need only a few minutes under the broiler.

Per piece: about
- 63 calories
- 2 g fat
- 2 g protein
- 10 g carbohydrate

2 tbsp	freshly grated Parmesan cheese	25 mL
2 tbsp	light mayonnaise	25 mL
1	clove garlic, minced	1
1/2 tsp	dried oregano	2 mL
12	slices baguette (French stick)	12
Half	small sweet red pepper, diced	Half

● In small bowl, stir together Parmesan cheese, mayonnaise, garlic and oregano; spread evenly over bread. Sprinkle with red pepper. Broil on rimmed baking sheet for 2 to 3 minutes or until golden. Makes 12 pieces.

Leek and Brie Pizza Fingers

Pizza comes bite-size using convenient store-bought flatbread as the starting point.

Per piece: about
- 81 calories
- 5 g fat
- 3 g protein
- 7 g carbohydrate

3 tbsp	butter	50 mL
6 cups	thinly sliced trimmed leeks	1.5 L
2/3 cup	whipping cream	150 mL
1/3 cup	freshly grated Parmesan cheese	75 mL
Pinch	each salt and pepper	Pinch
1	long flatbread, cut in half	1
4 oz	Brie cheese, cut in bits	125 g
	Chopped fresh parsley	

● In large heavy saucepan, melt butter over medium-low heat; cook leeks, stirring occasionally, for 15 minutes or until softened but not browned.

● Add cream and bring to boil; boil, stirring frequently, for 2 minutes or until thickened and reduced by half. Stir in Parmesan cheese, salt and pepper.

● Spread leek mixture over bread; scatter Brie over top. Bake on baking sheets in 400°F (200°C) oven for about 12 minutes or until crust is crisped and cheese melted. Sprinkle with parsley to taste. Cut into fingers to serve. Makes about 30 pieces.

Toasted Mushroom Bread

Here's a jumbo mushroom melt sure to satisfy a whole team of eaters. It originated with Kristen Sprague, Olympic athlete and wife of baseball player Ed Sprague, as her contribution to recipes in Canadian Living *and The Blue Jays.*

Per piece: about
- 187 calories
- 10 g fat
- 6 g protein
- 18 g carbohydrate

1	large round bread loaf (French or Italian sourdough)	1
1/2 cup	butter, softened	125 mL
5 cups	thinly sliced mushrooms (about 1 lb/500 g)	1.25 L
2 cups	shredded mozzarella cheese	500 mL
8	green onions, finely chopped	8
3	cloves garlic, pressed	3

● Slice bread in half horizontally. With fingers, pull out about one-third of the soft bread; reserve for another use such as bread crumbs.

● In bowl, beat butter until smooth; stir in mushrooms. Mix in cheese, onions and garlic; spread on both cut sides of bread. Place, cut side up, on baking sheet.

● Bake in 400°F (200°C) oven for 10 to 15 minutes or until crisp on outside and cheese is melted. Cut each into 8 wedges; cut in half again. Makes 16 pieces.

SPRING ANTIPASTO PLATTER

Garlic Cheese Toasts (p. 10) star in a springtime entertaining platter that's easy to assemble and impressive to behold. Here's how to create an amazing collection of delectables — some from the deli and some homemade — on your most attractive platter or tray.

● Start with Belgian endive leaves: they're holders par excellence. Arrange them around a platter and either fill them with slices of bocconcini and a few fresh herbs, or crumple paper-thin slices of prosciutto or Black Forest ham and fit them along the curve of the leaves. Then nestle in cherry tomatoes, olives if you like, roasted asparagus and, at the last moment, Garlic Cheese Toasts.

● To roast asparagus, arrange thick asparagus spears on rimmed baking sheet; sprinkle with a little olive oil, salt and pepper. Roast in 500°F (260°C) oven, turning spears once, for about 8 minutes or until tender but still slightly firm.

Crostini con Funghi ▲

Per piece: about
- 57 calories
- 2 g fat
- 2 g protein
- 8 g carbohydrate

3 tbsp	olive oil	50 mL
1	onion, thinly sliced	1
2	cloves garlic, minced	2
12 oz	mixed sliced mushrooms	375 g
1/4 cup	sliced sweet red pepper	50 mL
1/4 cup	dry white wine	50 mL
2 tbsp	chopped capers	25 mL
1 tbsp	chopped fresh parsley	15 mL
2 tsp	chopped fresh thyme (or 1/2 tsp/2 mL dried)	10 mL
1/4 tsp	each salt and pepper	1 mL
1	tomato, seeded and chopped	1
1	stick Italian bread	1

● In large skillet, heat oil over medium-high heat; cook onion and garlic, stirring often, for 5 to 7 minutes or until softened and lightly golden. Stir in mushrooms; cook for about 7 minutes or until softened and lightly browned.

● Stir in red pepper, wine, capers, parsley and thyme; cook for 3 minutes or until peppers are just softened. Remove from heat; stir in salt, pepper and tomato.

● Meanwhile, slice bread into 24 rounds; toast lightly. Top each with about 2 tbsp (25 mL) mushroom mixture. Makes 24 pieces.

TIP: You can make Crostini con Funghi using only regular mushrooms. However, a combination of different types makes it extra-special: shiitake, portobello, porcini and button mushrooms would be a good mixture.

Chèvre and Roasted Pepper Bruschetta

1	baguette (French stick)	1
1	sweet red pepper	1
1/2 cup	cream goat cheese (chèvre)	125 mL
1 tsp	(approx) olive oil	5 mL
1/2 tsp	dried basil (or 2 tsp/10 mL chopped fresh)	2 mL
	Pepper	
	Minced fresh parsley	

● Slice bread 3/4 inch (2 cm) thick to make 18 rounds; broil on baking sheet for 1 to 2 minutes or just until lightly browned. *(Toasts can be stored in airtight container for up to 24 hours.)*

● Broil red pepper, turning several times, for about 20 minutes or until blistered and charred. Let cool. Peel, core, seed and chop; place in bowl. Add cheese, oil, basil, and pepper to taste; mix well, adding up to 1 tsp (5 mL) more oil if necessary to make spreadable. *(Cheese mixture can be refrigerated in airtight container for up to 24 hours.)*

● Turn toasts over; spread heaping 1 tsp (5 mL) on untoasted side. Broil 6 inches (15 cm) from heat, watching closely, for 1-1/2 to 2 minutes or until hot. Sprinkle with parsley to taste. Makes 18 pieces.

Busy entertainers take note — this vibrantly colored and flavored appetizer can be made ahead, then assembled and run under the broiler at the last minute (photo, p. 7).

Per piece: about
- 70 calories
- 2 g fat
- 3 g protein
- 10 g carbohydrate

Shrimp Croustades

1	loaf (675 g) sliced whole wheat or white bread	1
1 tbsp	butter	15 mL
1	green onion, sliced	1
2 tbsp	all-purpose flour	25 mL
3/4 cup	milk	175 mL
1/2 cup	shredded extra-old Cheddar or Swiss cheese	125 mL
1-1/2 cups	coarsely chopped cooked shrimp	375 mL
1 tbsp	minced fresh parsley	15 mL
2 tsp	grated lemon rind	10 mL
2 tsp	lemon juice	10 mL
Dash	each Worcestershire sauce and hot pepper sauce	Dash
Pinch	each salt and pepper	Pinch
	Paprika	

● Using 2-inch (5 cm) round cookie cutter, cut out about 60 circles from bread slices; reserve trimmings for another use such as bread crumbs. Press each firmly into mini tart cups to form shells. Bake in 450°F

(230°C) oven for 5 to 8 minutes or until lightly browned and crisp. Transfer croustades to baking sheet; set aside.

● In small saucepan, melt butter over medium heat; cook onion, stirring occasionally, for 3 to 5 minutes or until softened. Stir in flour until blended; gradually whisk in milk and cook, stirring, for 2 to 4 minutes or until boiling and thickened. Stir in cheese until melted. Stir in shrimp, parsley, lemon rind and juice, Worcestershire sauce, hot pepper sauce, salt and pepper.

● Mound about 1 tsp (5 mL) filling into each croustade; sprinkle lightly with paprika to taste. *(Croustades can be prepared to this point and frozen on baking sheet; layer between waxed paper and store in freezer in rigid airtight container for up to 2 weeks.)*

● Bake in 400°F (200°C) oven for 5 to 8 minutes, 15 minutes for frozen, or until filling is browned and bubbly. Makes 60 pieces.

You'll be tempted to have "just one more" of these golden seafood cups (photo, p. 7). Because they go from freezer to guests in just 15 minutes, it's easy to keep the party supplied.

Per piece: about
- 24 calories
- 1 g fat
- 2 g protein
- 3 g carbohydrate

Brie Walnut Toast Cups ▼

Use only fresh California walnuts for these creamy tartlets. Because whole walnut halves are usually of superior quality, buy the nuts that way, store them in the freezer and chop them to order.

Per piece: about
- 35 calories
- 2 g fat
- 1 g protein
- 3 g carbohydrate

1/2 cup	chopped walnuts	125 mL
6 oz	Brie cheese	175 g
2 oz	light cream cheese	60 g
1	egg	1
1/4 tsp	pepper	1 mL
60	Toast Cups (recipe, p. 15)	60

● Spread walnuts on baking sheet; toast in 350°F (180°C) oven for 5 to 7 minutes or until golden. Let cool.

● Remove rind from Brie; cut cheese into small cubes. In bowl, beat together Brie and cream cheeses; beat in egg. Stir in 1/4 cup (50 mL) of the walnuts and pepper.

● Place Toast Cups in 1-1/2-inch (4 cm) tart tins; fill each with 1 tsp (5 mL) cheese mixture. *(Appetizers can be prepared to this point, covered and refrigerated for up to 24 hours.)*

● Sprinkle filling with remaining walnuts; bake in 300°F (150°C) oven for 15 to 20 minutes or until heated through. Makes 60 pieces.

Asparagus Cheese, Dilled Shrimp and Brie Walnut Toast Cups

Dilled Shrimp Toast Cups ◄

1/4 cup	mayonnaise	50 mL
1 tbsp	(approx) finely chopped fresh dill	15 mL
1 tsp	finely grated lemon rind	5 mL
2 tsp	lemon juice	10 mL
8 oz	tiny cooked salad shrimp	250 g
24	Toast Cups (recipe, this page)	24
24	fresh dill sprigs	24

● In bowl, stir together mayonnaise, chopped dill, lemon rind and juice; season with more dill to taste, if desired. Add shrimp; toss gently to combine.

● Fill each Toast Cup with 2 tsp (10 mL) shrimp mixture. Garnish each with dill sprig. Makes 24 pieces.

Not many guests can resist shrimp, especially served in this classic way.

Per piece: about
- 45 calories
- 3 g fat
- 3 g protein
- 3 g carbohydrate

Asparagus Cheese Toast Cups ◄

5	stalks asparagus	5
24	Toast Cups (recipe, this page)	24
1 tbsp	Dijon mustard	15 mL
3/4 cup	shredded provolone or mozzarella cheese	175 mL

● Slice asparagus into 1/4-inch (5 mm) thick rounds. Place Toast Cups in 1-1/2-inch (4 cm) tart tins. Brush evenly with mustard; mound cheese in cups. Top each with 3 asparagus rounds. *(Appetizers can be prepared to this point, covered and refrigerated for up to 1 day.)*

● Bake in 300°F (150°C) oven for 15 to 20 minutes or until cheese melts. Makes 24 pieces.

Toast cups crisp around a combo of sprightly green asparagus and melted provolone cheese.

Per piece: about
- 33 calories
- 2 g fat
- 2 g protein
- 3 g carbohydrate

VERSATILE TOAST CUPS

Bite-size toast cups are perfect for parties — they're easier to make than pastry and easier to eat. Best of all, they don't crumble! They're also lower in calories and less expensive. Make them days or weeks ahead and serve hot or cold.

● Trim crusts from 1 loaf sliced bread; roll each slice until about 1/8 inch (3 mm) thick. Using 2-inch (5 cm) round cookie cutter, cut 2 circles from each slice to make about 40 rounds; reserve trimmings for another use such as bread crumbs.
● Brush rounds lightly with 1 tbsp (15 mL) vegetable oil. Tuck into 1-1/2-inch (4 cm) tart tins to form shells; bake in 350°F (180°C) oven for 10 to 15 minutes or until crisp and light golden brown. Let cool on racks. *(Toast cups can be stored in airtight container for up to 1 week or frozen for up to 1 month.)* Makes 40 toast cups.

Per toast cup: about • 20 calories • 1 g protein • 1 g fat • 3 g carbohydrate

Curried Chicken Crunchies ▶

Appetizers are meant to sing with flavor, and this curry chicken stir-fry, its spicy edges mellowed with mayo and yogurt, is a chorus. Corn chips provide a novel base for such a topping.

Per piece: about
- 30 calories
- 2 g protein
- 1 g fat
- 2 g carbohydrate

2	boneless skinless chicken breasts	2
3/4 tsp	curry powder	4 mL
1/2 tsp	turmeric	2 mL
1/4 tsp	each ground cumin and coriander	1 mL
Pinch	each salt and pepper	Pinch
2 tsp	vegetable oil	10 mL
2 tbsp	plain yogurt	25 mL
2 tbsp	light mayonnaise	25 mL
24	round corn chips	24
4	radishes, thinly sliced	4
	Fresh chives	

● Cut chicken into 1/2-inch (1 cm) pieces. Combine curry powder, turmeric, cumin, coriander, salt and pepper. In nonstick skillet, heat oil over medium heat; stir-fry spice mixture for 1 minute. Add chicken; cook, stirring, for about 5 minutes or until no longer pink inside. Remove from skillet; let cool. *(Chicken can be covered and refrigerated for up to 24 hours.)*

● In bowl, combine chicken, yogurt and mayonnaise. Place 1 or 2 chicken pieces on each corn chip; garnish with radishes and chives. Makes 24 pieces.

Shrimp Canapés ▶

Open-face sandwiches are an open invitation to sample, especially when a tasty shrimp rests on top.

Per piece: about
- 70 calories
- 4 g protein
- 2 g fat
- 9 g carbohydrate

12	large shrimp, peeled and deveined	12
12	slices pumpernickel cocktail bread	12
12	slices unpeeled English cucumber	12
3 tbsp	light mayonnaise	50 mL
1 tbsp	chopped fresh chives	15 mL
1/2 tsp	lemon juice	2 mL
Pinch	each salt and pepper	Pinch
	Fresh chives and lemon slices	

● In pot of simmering salted water, poach shrimp for 2 to 3 minutes or just until pink. Drain well and let cool. *(Shrimp can be covered and refrigerated for up to 8 hours.)*

● Place bread slices on serving tray; top each with cucumber slice, then shrimp. In small bowl, stir together mayonnaise, chopped chives, lemon juice, salt and pepper; dot onto each bread slice beside shrimp. Garnish with chives and lemon. Makes 12 pieces.

PARTY SANDWICHES

Party sandwiches — that splendid array of one-bite rectangles, pinwheels, two-tone ribbons, checkerboards and artfully cut diamonds — are as popular as ever. But you can put together a pleasing platterful even without the fancy fillings.

● Well-seasoned egg, tuna and salmon salad, shaved deli meats (especially roast beef, smoky hams and turkey with Dijon mayonnaise) and classic standbys such as cucumber and watercress are sure to make mouths water.

● Boost the appeal of cream cheese with pesto, olives, sun-dried tomatoes or fresh herbs. Splurge on enough smoked salmon to add dazzle to the selection.

● Nor do you have to go crazy making fancy pinwheels and checkerboards — although cutting out hearts, bells and shamrock shapes is fun for celebrations and special occasions. Just make sure the bread is fresh and crusts are trimmed, then cut the sandwiches into neat fingers or triangles.

● Mini pita breads, baguettes and plain or colored tortillas also make tasty and attractive holders for an assortment of fillings.

Carrot Salad Bites ▼

1-1/2 cups	grated carrots	375 mL
1 tbsp	lemon juice	15 mL
1 tbsp	olive oil	15 mL
Pinch	each salt and pepper	Pinch
12	slices rye cocktail bread	12
1/3 cup	herbed cream cheese	75 mL
	Parsley sprigs	
	Violas or chive flowers (optional)	

● In bowl, stir together carrots, lemon juice, oil, salt and pepper. *(Filling can be covered and refrigerated for up to 24 hours.)*

● Place bread slices on serving tray; spread cream cheese over each. Divide carrot mixture among slices. Garnish with parsley, and violas (if using). Makes 12 pieces.

Take an everyday ingredient such as carrots and turn it into a stunning and simply delicious appetizer.

Per piece: about
- 80 calories
- 4 g fat
- 2 g protein
- 10 g carbohydrate

(Clockwise from top) Grilled Salmon Waves (p. 83), Shrimp Canapés (p. 16), Maritime Crab Cakes (p. 87), Carrot Salad Bites, Curried Chicken Crunchies (p. 16)

Smoked Turkey and Chutney Sandwiches

It's the smoke that stands up to assertive chutney, and you can get it from deli-available turkey, chicken or always-popular ham.

Per piece: about
- 58 calories
- 2 g fat
- 3 g protein
- 7 g carbohydrate

8 oz	light cream cheese	250 g
3 tbsp	mango chutney	50 mL
2 tbsp	lemon juice	25 mL
1/2 tsp	finely grated orange rind	2 mL
12 oz	thinly sliced smoked turkey	375 g
	Pepper	
22	slices sandwich loaf	22

● In large bowl, blend together cream cheese, chutney, lemon juice and orange rind until smooth. Cut turkey into slivers; stir into cheese mixture. Season with pepper to taste. *(Filling can be covered and refrigerated for up to 3 days; bring to room temperature.)*

● Spread half of the bread slices with filling; sandwich with remaining bread. Trim off crusts. Cut each sandwich into 4 pieces. Makes 44 pieces.

Mini Beef-and-Cress Sandwiches

Rare or medium rare is simply the best for roast beef sandwiches, and ask for very thinly sliced so the meat drapes softly on the bread.

Per piece: about
- 73 calories
- 4 g fat
- 3 g protein
- 6 g carbohydrate

1/2 cup	butter, softened	125 mL
2 tbsp	well-drained horseradish	25 mL
1 tsp	lemon juice	5 mL
Pinch	dry mustard	Pinch
1	22-inch (55 cm) baguette (French stick)	1
8 oz	thinly sliced roast beef	250 g
1	bunch watercress	1

● In small bowl, beat together butter, horseradish, lemon juice and mustard. *(Spread can be covered and refrigerated for up to 3 days; bring to room temperature.)*

● Using very sharp knife, slice baguette into 1/4-inch (5 mm) thick slices; spread with horseradish mixture. Cut roast beef into pieces; place on half of the slices. Top with sprig of watercress and remaining baguette slices. *(Sandwiches can be wrapped in plastic wrap, covered with damp tea towel and refrigerated for up to 3 hours.)* Makes about 30 pieces.

Egg and Watercress Sandwiches

A flavorful basic egg salad is the start for all kinds of tasty party sandwiches. Here, forest-green watercress and white and brown bread create a pretty ribbon effect.

Per piece: about
- 63 calories
- 4 g fat
- 2 g protein
- 4 g carbohydrate

10	hard-cooked eggs	10
1/2 cup	mayonnaise	125 mL
3	green onions, chopped	3
1/2 tsp	Worcestershire sauce	2 mL
	Salt and pepper	
1/3 cup	butter, softened	75 mL
8	slices brown sandwich loaf	8
8	slices white sandwich loaf	8
2 cups	watercress	500 mL

● In bowl, mash eggs with mayonnaise until blended. Stir in green onions and Worcestershire sauce. Season with salt and pepper to taste.

● Evenly spread butter over brown and white bread. Spread egg filling evenly to edges of white bread. Top with watercress and brown bread. *(Sandwiches can be wrapped in plastic wrap, covered with damp tea towel and refrigerated for up to 24 hours.)*

● Trim off crusts. Cut sandwiches crosswise into halves; cut each half into 3 rectangles. Makes 48 pieces.

Blockbuster Burger Bites ▲

2	eggs	2
2 tbsp	water	25 mL
1/2 cup	dry bread crumbs	125 mL
1	onion, grated	1
2 tsp	Dijon mustard	10 mL
2 tsp	Worcestershire sauce	10 mL
1/2 tsp	each salt and pepper	2 mL
2 lb	lean ground beef	1 kg
16	mini hamburger buns or dinner rolls (3 inches/8 cm)	16

● In bowl, whisk eggs with water; mix in bread crumbs, onion, mustard, Worcestershire sauce, salt and pepper. Using fork, mix in beef. Shape into sixteen 1/4-inch (5 mm) thick patties. Place on foil-lined baking sheet. *(Patties can be covered with plastic wrap and refrigerated for up to 8 hours.)*

● Broil patties, turning once, for about 10 minutes or until no longer pink inside. Cut buns in half; place burgers in between. Makes 16 pieces.

TOP THAT!
Offer a selection of toppings so that guests can customize their burgers. Set out in bowls and let everyone create their own winning combos.
● Tasty toppers include chopped roasted red peppers, alfalfa sprouts, diced avocado, guacamole, cream goat cheese, prepared pesto, thinly sliced plum tomatoes, sliced dill pickles, shredded lettuce, thinly sliced old Cheddar cheese, crumbled cooked bacon and thinly sliced red onion.

N*ext time the gang gathers for a Friday-night video party, put out a platter of these fifties-style mini burgers along with bowlfuls of today's most popular toppings.*

Per piece: about
● 255 calories ● 16 g protein
● 9 g fat ● 26 g carbohydrate

(Clockwise from top) Tortilla Roll-Ups (p. 64), Mini Bagel Beef Rounds, Mini Beef Pita Pockets (p. 21)

Mini Bagel Beef Rounds ▲

When the occasion calls for something small but satisfying, these mini sandwiches fit the bill nicely.

Per appetizer: about
- 225 calories
- 7 g fat
- good source of iron
- 13 g protein
- 27 g carbohydrate

6	mini bagels	6
1/4 cup	light mayonnaise	50 mL
1 tbsp	minced green onion	15 mL
2 tsp	Dijon mustard	10 mL
2	lettuce leaves	2
6	thin slices tomato	6
6	thin slices cooked roast beef	6

● Slice bagels in half horizontally. In small bowl, stir together mayonnaise, onion and mustard; spread evenly over cut sides of bagels. Tear each lettuce leaf into 3; place on bottom halves of bagels. Top with tomato, then beef. Sandwich with remaining bagel halves. *(Sandwiches can be covered and refrigerated for up to 4 hours.)* Makes 6 appetizers.

Mini Beef Pita Pockets ◀

6	mini pita breads	6
2 tbsp	light mayonnaise	25 mL
2 tsp	pesto	10 mL
3	thin slices cooked roast beef	3
6	thin slices cucumber	6
1/2 cup	sweet red pepper strips or alfalfa sprouts	125 mL

● Slice off top of each pita to form pocket. In small bowl, stir mayonnaise with pesto; spread evenly over insides of pockets. Dividing evenly, insert beef, cucumbers and red pepper strip in each. *(Pitas can be covered and refrigerated for up to 1 hour.)* Makes 6 appetizers.

For a change of taste, substitute sun-dried tomato pesto for the regular basil.

Per appetizer: about
- 75 calories
- 4 g fat
- 5 g protein
- 5 g carbohydrate

Black Olive Mini Pita Pockets

6 oz	cream cheese	175 g
2 oz	feta cheese, rinsed	60 g
1/4 cup	chopped black olives	50 mL
1 tsp	finely grated lemon rind	5 mL
2 tbsp	lemon juice	25 mL
12	mini pita breads	12
	Leaf lettuce	

● In bowl, blend cream cheese with feta cheese; stir in olives, lemon rind and juice. *(Filling can be covered and refrigerated for up to 24 hours; bring to room temperature.)*

● Cut pitas in half; open to form pockets. Line each with piece of lettuce; spoon 2 tsp (10 mL) filling into each. Makes 24 pieces.

Lining mini pitas with lettuce adds fresh crunch and waterproofs the bread.

Per piece: about
- 44 calories
- 3 g fat
- 1 g protein
- 3 g carbohydrate

PICK-UP BREAD BITES

Here are some quick solutions to the no-time-but-love-to-entertain situations so many of us find ourselves in. Look to the delicious bread products found in many stores and complement them with other pick-up ingredients such as marinated vegetables, olives, cheese with presence, smoky meats or fish or fresh produce such as radishes, cherry tomatoes or sugar snap peas.

● For an instant appetizer with presence, wrap one end of breadsticks with thinly sliced prosciutto.

● Brush pita breads or tortillas lightly with olive oil; sprinkle with a favorite herb and bake in single layer on baking sheets in 350°F (180°C) oven until crisp.

● Make Cheesy Crostini (featured on cover) in minutes. Cut white sandwich bread into attractive shapes or rounds with cookie cutter. Top with slice of mozzarella or other melty cheese. Garnish with cherry tomato slice; sprinkle with pepper or your favorite herbs. Bake in single layer on baking sheet in 350°F (175°C) oven until crisp and cheese is melted.

● Make the most of freezer or refrigerator yeast doughs. For quick focaccia, roll out dough as directed. Brush with oil and sprinkle generously with Italian seasonings, herbes de Provence or simply fresh or dried sage, basil or rosemary. A light sprinkle of Parmesan (real Parmigiano Reggiano) is a good idea, too.

To serve, cut into wedges or fingers.

● Make an interactive some-assembly-needed tray with tortillas, cream cheese or goat cheese and a selection of zesty ingredients such as chutney, salsa, pesto, pitted olives, crab, shrimp, smoked mussels or oysters, salami, roasted red peppers, oil-packed sun-dried tomatoes and fresh herbs.

● Do the same Chinese-style with tortillas, hoisin sauce, barbecued pork and fresh bean sprouts — or go Middle Eastern with mini pita breads to fill with hummus, tzatziki or other Greek or Middle Eastern dips available commercially, plus feta, chopped tomatoes and/or pitted olives.

● Try rye bread, cocktail size if possible, light cream cheese, smoked trout or mackerel (without the skin), lemon slices and capers. When feeling flush, set out smoked salmon or golden (whitefish) caviar. For a sure pleaser, offer rye slices with shaved Black Forest ham, mustard and dills.

Party Lobster Pockets

This mini version of a Maritime specialty is so good it will find takers across the country.

Per piece: about
- 46 calories
- 1 g fat
- 3 g protein
- 6 g carbohydrate

1	can (320 g/11.3 oz) frozen lobster meat, thawed	1
1/2 cup	each chopped celery and radishes	125 mL
1/2 cup	diced carrot	125 mL
1/4 cup	finely chopped green onions	50 mL
1/2 cup	light mayonnaise	125 mL
1/3 cup	light sour cream	75 mL
2 tbsp	chopped fresh dill	25 mL
1 tbsp	lemon juice	15 mL
Dash	hot pepper sauce	Dash
	Salt and pepper	
36	mini pita breads	36
	Leaf lettuce	

● Drain lobster and squeeze dry; shred into bowl. Add celery, radishes, carrot and green onions. *(Filling can be covered and refrigerated for up to 1 day; drain before continuing.)*

● In bowl, stir together mayonnaise, sour cream, dill, lemon juice and hot pepper sauce; stir into lobster mixture. Season with salt and pepper to taste. Slit opening in pitas; line with lettuce. Spoon in lobster mixture. *(Pockets can be covered with plastic wrap and refrigerated for up to 2 hours.)* Makes 36 pieces.

Mini Herb Scones with Red Pepper Frittata

Eggs needn't be just for breakfast. Whipped up as an easy-fix frittata and tucked into tiny scones, they find a niche as an any-time-of-day appetizer. If you like, spread the scones lightly with a little pesto, cream cheese or mayo before filling with the frittata.

Per piece: about
- 68 calories
- 4 g fat
- 2 g protein
- 7 g carbohydrate

1/4 cup	finely diced sweet red pepper	50 mL
1	green onion, thinly sliced	1
2	eggs	2
1 tbsp	milk	15 mL
Pinch	each salt and pepper	Pinch
	Leaf lettuce	
	SCONES	
1 cup	all-purpose flour	250 mL
1 tbsp	granulated sugar	15 mL
1 tsp	baking powder	5 mL
1/2 tsp	dried basil	2 mL
1/4 tsp	salt	1 mL
1/4 cup	cold butter, cubed	50 mL
1/3 cup	milk	75 mL
1 tbsp	butter, melted	15 mL

● Spread red pepper and green onion in lightly greased 7-inch (18 cm) ovenproof skillet or pie plate. In bowl, whisk together eggs, milk, salt and pepper; pour into skillet. Bake in 375°F (190°C) oven for 8 minutes or until set in middle and edge is puffed. Gently loosen from skillet. Let cool in skillet on rack to room temperature.

● SCONES: Meanwhile, in bowl, stir together flour, sugar, baking powder, basil and salt. Using pastry blender or two knives, cut in butter until in tiny pieces with a few larger ones. Add milk all at once; stir with fork to make soft sticky dough.

● Turn out dough onto lightly floured surface; knead 8 to 10 times or just until smooth. Gently roll out to 1/2-inch (1 cm) thickness. Using 1-1/2-inch (4 cm) round cookie cutter, cut out scones; roll out and cut scraps once, pressing dough together to avoid rerolling.

● Place scones on ungreased baking sheet. Brush tops with melted butter. Bake in center of 400°F (200°C) oven for 12 to 15 minutes or until puffed and golden. Let cool on pan on rack for 5 minutes.

● Turn frittata out of skillet onto cutting board. Cut into 4 strips; cut diagonally into triangular pieces 1-1/2 inches (4 cm) long. Cut scones in half horizontally. Place piece of lettuce and frittata on each bottom piece; replace tops. Makes 18 pieces.

Turkey Sweet Potato Scone Sandwiches ▲

1/4 cup	cranberry sauce	50 mL
4 tsp	sweet mustard	20 mL
3 oz	sliced smoked turkey	90 g
3	leaves Bibb or Boston lettuce	3
	SWEET POTATO SCONES	
1	large sweet potato (about 12 oz/375 g)	1
1/4 cup	milk	50 mL
1 cup	all-purpose flour	250 mL
2/3 cup	whole wheat flour	150 mL
4 tsp	granulated sugar	20 mL
1 tbsp	baking powder	15 mL
1/4 tsp	salt	1 mL
1/3 cup	cold butter, cubed	75 mL

● SWEET POTATO SCONES: Prick sweet potato all over with fork; microwave at High, turning twice, for about 12 minutes or until tender. (Or bake in 400°F/200°C oven for 1 hour and 15 minutes.) Let cool slightly. Scoop out pulp into bowl; mash until smooth to make 3/4 cup (175 mL). Stir in milk. Set aside.

● In separate bowl, stir together all-purpose and whole wheat flours, sugar, baking powder and salt. Using pastry blender or two knives, cut in butter until in tiny pieces with a few larger ones. Using fork, stir in potato mixture just until shaggy dough forms.

● Turn out dough onto lightly floured surface; knead lightly 8 to 10 times or just until smooth. Gently pat into 3/4-inch (2 cm) thick disc. Using 2-inch (5 cm) round cookie cutter, cut out scones; pat out and cut scraps once, pressing dough together to avoid rerolling.

● Place scones on ungreased baking sheet. Bake in center of 400°F (200°C) oven for 15 to 18 minutes or until puffed and bottoms are golden. Let cool on pan on rack for about 5 minutes. Transfer to rack; let cool completely.

● Split each scone in half horizontally. Spread cut side of bottom halves with cranberry sauce; spread tops with mustard. Layer turkey and lettuce over cranberry sauce; sandwich with top half of scone. Makes 12 pieces.

Once the darling of afternoon tea, scones have been updated with new flavors, fillings and mini size to find a genuine welcome as brunch and pre-dinner appetizer bites.

Per piece: about
• 162 calories
• 6 g fat
• 4 g protein
• 23 g carbohydrate

Pâtés and Cheese

Our superlative pâtés and savory cheese cakes, rolls and rounds are the perfect entertaining solution to an evening of nibbles and wine.

Pâté Maison ▶

While there's no denying that making your own pâté is work, homemade costs a fraction of the price of bought, is make-ahead and fuss-free to serve. All in all, an excellent and impressive appetizer for large gatherings.

Per serving: about
- 109 calories
- 6 g fat
- 11 g protein
- 2 g carbohydrate

3 tbsp	butter	50 mL
1 cup	diced onion	250 mL
4	cloves garlic, minced	4
12 oz	chicken livers, trimmed and halved	375 g
12 oz	each ground pork and ground veal	375 g
4 oz	smoked ham, diced	125 g
1/4 cup	dry sherry or chicken stock	50 mL
1	egg, beaten	1
1-1/2 tsp	each salt and pepper	7 mL
1 tsp	Dijon mustard	5 mL
3/4 tsp	dried thyme	4 mL
1/2 tsp	nutmeg	2 mL
3	bay leaves	3
3 tbsp	cracked peppercorns	50 mL

● In skillet, melt butter over medium-high heat; cook onion and garlic, stirring occasionally, for 3 minutes or until softened. Add chicken livers; cook, stirring often, for 5 minutes or until just slightly pink inside. Let cool for 5 minutes.

● In food processor or blender, purée chicken liver mixture until smooth. Transfer to large bowl. Add pork, veal, ham, sherry, egg, salt, pepper, mustard, thyme and nutmeg; mix well.

● Pack into greased 9- x 5-inch (2 L) loaf pan; arrange bay leaves over top. Tap pan on counter to remove air bubbles. Cover tightly with foil; place in larger pan. Pour enough water into larger pan to come halfway up sides. Bake in 350°F (180°C) oven for about 2 hours or until meat thermometer registers 160° to 170°F (70° to 75°C).

● Discard bay leaves; pour off any juices. Let cool, covered, for 30 minutes. Refrigerate for at least 12 hours or for up to 48 hours. To serve, let stand at room temperature for 30 minutes; unmould onto serving platter. Coat top with peppercorns. Makes 20 servings.

TIPS
- For a touch of crunch, add chopped nuts such as hazelnuts or pistachios when mixing in the meats.
- To crack peppercorns, place between sheets of waxed paper on cutting board and smash with rolling pin or bottom of saucepan.
- Garnish servings with seasonal fruits such as fresh figs or the new kiwi grapes.
- Serve pâté with a tangy relish or fruit chutney and with toasted bread, crusts trimmed off and cut into quarters.

Lighter-than-Most Mushroom and Liver Pâté

Liver pâtés are undeniably delicious but notoriously high in fat. Not wanting to lessen any of the rich taste and creamy texture that makes pâtés so popular, the Canadian Living Test Kitchen bulked up and browned the mushrooms and buzzed the blend so well you don't miss any of the butter and cream.

Per tbsp (15 mL): about
- 20 calories
- 2 g protein
- 1 g fat
- 1 g carbohydrate

2 tbsp	butter	25 mL
2	cloves garlic, minced	2
2	stalks celery, chopped	2
1	onion, chopped	1
1-1/2 tsp	dried thyme	7 mL
1 tsp	dried basil	5 mL
2 tbsp	white wine vinegar	25 mL
1-1/3 lb	coarsely chopped mushrooms	670 g
8 oz	chicken livers, trimmed and halved	250 g
1/4 cup	light cream cheese, softened	50 mL
1/2 tsp	each salt and pepper	2 mL
1 tbsp	chopped fresh parsley	15 mL

● In large nonstick skillet, heat half of the butter over medium heat; cook garlic, celery, onion, thyme and basil, stirring occasionally, for about 5 minutes or until onions are softened. Stir in vinegar; cook until evaporated.

● Increase heat to medium-high. Add mushrooms; cook, stirring often, for about 15 minutes or until browned. Transfer to bowl; let cool completely.

● In same skillet, melt remaining butter over medium heat; cook chicken livers, stirring, for about 5 minutes or until just slightly pink inside. Let stand for 5 minutes.

● In food processor or blender, purée together mushroom mixture, chicken livers, cream cheese, salt and pepper until smooth. Scrape into serving bowl. Cover and refrigerate for at least 4 hours or until firm. *(Pâté can be refrigerated for up to 2 days.)* Sprinkle with parsley. Makes about 2-1/2 cups (625 mL).

Mushroom and Leek Pâté

Welcome guests, as does author and food writer Dana McCauley, with this light vegetarian pâté. Serve with water crackers or toasted flatbreads.

Per each of 8 servings: about
- 95 calories
- 3 g protein
- 7 g fat
- 6 g carbohydrate

2 tbsp	butter	25 mL
1 cup	thinly sliced leeks or onions	250 mL
1/2 cup	chopped celery	125 mL
2	cloves garlic, minced	2
1-1/2 tsp	dried thyme	7 mL
1/2 tsp	pepper	2 mL
Pinch	salt	Pinch
2 tbsp	sherry	25 mL
1 tsp	Worcestershire sauce	5 mL
1-1/2 lb	coarsely chopped mushrooms	750 g
2 tbsp	tomato paste	25 mL
4 oz	light cream cheese, softened	125 g
2 tbsp	chopped fresh parsley	25 mL

● In large saucepan, melt butter over medium heat; cook leeks, celery, garlic, thyme, pepper and salt, stirring occasionally, for 10 minutes or until leeks are softened and lightly browned. Stir in sherry and Worcestershire sauce; cook for 30 seconds, stirring to scrape up any brown bits from bottom of pan.

● Increase heat to high. Add mushrooms; cook, stirring occasionally, for about 10 minutes or until liquid is evaporated. Stir in tomato paste; cook for 1 minute. Let cool to room temperature.

● In food processor or blender, mix cream cheese with mushroom mixture just until almost smooth. Sprinkle parsley evenly over bottom of 2-cup (500 mL) plastic wrap-lined loaf pan or mould. Spoon in mushroom mixture, smoothing top. Cover and refrigerate for at least 4 hours or until firm. *(Pâté can be refrigerated for up to 3 days.)* Unmould onto serving platter; smooth with palette knife. Makes 6 to 8 servings.

Chilled Vegetable Terrine with Parsley Sauce ▼

2	pkg (7 g each) unflavored gelatin	2
1/2 cup	cold water	125 mL
4	large carrots (1 lb/500 g), sliced	4
1/2 tsp	dried dillweed	2 mL
3/4 tsp	each salt and pepper	4 mL
1 cup	light mayonnaise	250 mL
1	pkg (10 oz/284 g) fresh spinach	1
2 tbsp	lemon juice	25 mL
Pinch	cayenne pepper	Pinch
4	large parsnips (1 lb/500 g), sliced	4
1/4 tsp	nutmeg	1 mL
	Parsley Sauce (recipe follows)	

● In small saucepan, sprinkle gelatin over cold water; let stand for 5 minutes. Heat over low heat, stirring, for 2 to 3 minutes or until dissolved.

● In saucepan of boiling water, cook carrots for about 15 minutes or until very tender. Drain and transfer to food processor; purée until smooth. Add dill, 1/4 tsp (1 mL) each of the salt and pepper, 1/3 cup (75 mL) of the mayonnaise and 3 tbsp (50 mL) of the gelatin mixture; blend well. Spoon into 8- by 4-inch (1.5 L) plastic wrap-lined loaf pan; refrigerate.

● Rinse spinach, shaking off excess water. In saucepan, cook spinach, with just the water clinging to leaves, for about 5 minutes or just until wilted. Drain and squeeze dry. Purée in food processor. Add 1/4 tsp (1 mL) each of the salt and pepper, 1/3 cup (75 mL) of the mayonnaise, 2 tbsp (25 mL) of the gelatin mixture, lemon juice and cayenne pepper; blend well. Spread over carrot layer; refrigerate.

● In saucepan of boiling water, cook parsnips for about 15 minutes or until very tender. Drain and transfer to food processor; purée until smooth. Add remaining salt, pepper, mayonnaise, gelatin mixture and

nutmeg; blend well. Spread over spinach layer. Cover and refrigerate for at least 8 hours or until chilled and set. *(Terrine can be refrigerated for up to 2 days.)* Unmould onto serving platter. Serve in slices with Parsley Sauce. Makes 8 servings.

PARSLEY SAUCE

1 cup	loosely packed fresh parsley leaves	250 mL
1/3 cup	vegetable oil	75 mL
2 tbsp	lemon juice	25 mL
1-1/2 tsp	Dijon mustard	7 mL
1/4 tsp	each salt and pepper	1 mL

● In food processor, chop parsley. Combine oil, lemon juice, mustard, salt and pepper. With motor running, add oil mixture, blending well. *(Sauce can be refrigerated in airtight container for up to 1 day.)* Makes 1/2 cup (125 mL).

This handsome terrine makes a spectacular starter course at any festive table. It was created by innkeeper Dominique Guilbeault from Compton, Quebec.

Per serving: about
- 261 calories
- 19 g fat
- high source of fiber
- 4 g protein
- 22 g carbohydrate
- good source of iron

TIP: Rewarm gelatin over low heat if it begins to set before finishing all layers.

Guacamole Pâté with Salsa ▲

*F*ood writer Bonnie Stern has made a reputation for herself because of her delicious and inventive recipes. Here's one that will add dazzle to your appetizer buffet table.

Per each of 12 servings: about
- 163 calories
- 3 g protein
- 15 g fat
- 6 g carbohydrate

1-1/2	pkg (7 g each) unflavored gelatin	1-1/2
2	ripe avocados, peeled and pitted	2
1 cup	sour cream	250 mL
1/2 cup	mayonnaise	125 mL
3 tbsp	lemon juice	50 mL
1/2 tsp	salt	2 mL
1/4 tsp	pepper	1 mL
Dash	hot pepper sauce	Dash
1	clove garlic, minced	1
1	small tomato, seeded and chopped	1
1	small jalapeño pepper, seeded and finely chopped	1
1/4 cup	chopped fresh coriander or parsley	50 mL
2	green onions, finely chopped	2
	SALSA	
1	each tomato, sweet red pepper and jalapeño pepper, seeded and chopped	1
2 tbsp	chopped fresh coriander or parsley	25 mL
2	green onions, chopped	2
1	clove garlic, minced	1

● In small saucepan, sprinkle gelatin over 1/4 cup (50 mL) cold water; let stand for 5 minutes. Heat over low heat, stirring, for 2 to 3 minutes or until dissolved.

● In food processor, purée together avocados, sour cream, mayonnaise, lemon juice, salt, pepper, hot pepper sauce and garlic until smooth; blend in dissolved gelatin. Stir in tomato, jalapeño pepper, coriander and onions.

● Spoon into 8- x 4-inch (1.5 L) plastic wrap-lined loaf pan; cover with plastic wrap. Refrigerate for 3 hours or until set. *(Pâté can be refrigerated for up to 24 hours.)*

● SALSA: In small bowl, combine tomato, red pepper, jalapeño pepper, coriander, onions and garlic. Unmould pâté onto serving platter; serve in slices with some salsa spooned down center of each. Makes 10 to 12 servings.

Double-Salmon Terrine ◄

2	cans (7 oz/213 g each) salmon, drained	2
8 oz	smoked salmon, diced	250 g
2 tbsp	chopped fresh parsley	25 mL
3	green onions, chopped	3
1 tsp	dried tarragon	5 mL
1/2 cup	butter, softened	125 mL
1/2 cup	mayonnaise	125 mL
1 tbsp	each Dijon mustard and lemon juice	15 mL
1/2 tsp	pepper	2 mL

● Flake salmon, discarding skin and bones. In bowl, gently combine flaked and smoked salmon, parsley, onions and tarragon.

● In separate bowl, beat together butter, mayonnaise, mustard, lemon juice and pepper; add salmon mixture and gently combine.

● Spoon into 8- x 4-inch (1.5 L) plastic wrap-lined loaf pan; cover with plastic wrap. Refrigerate for about 3 hours or until firm. *(Terrine can be refrigerated for up to 5 days or wrapped and frozen for up to 1 month.)* Unmould and serve in slices. Makes 12 to 15 servings.

Speckled with salmon, onion and parsley, this rich-tasting country-style pâté from food writer Bonnie Stern is perfect with slices of pumpernickel, multigrain bread or sourdough baguette.

Per each of 15 servings: about
- 161 calories
- 8 g protein
- 14 g fat
- 1 g carbohydrate

Smoked Salmon Pâté

1	pkg (7 g) unflavored gelatin	1
1/4 cup	cold water	50 mL
12 oz	smoked salmon	375 g
4 oz	cream cheese, softened	125 g
1 cup	sour cream	250 mL
2 tbsp	lemon juice	25 mL
1-1/2 cups	whipping cream	375 mL
	Salt and pepper	
1	pkg (10 oz/284 g) fresh spinach, cooked and squeezed dry	1

● In small saucepan, sprinkle gelatin over cold water; let stand for 5 minutes. Heat over low heat, stirring, for 2 to 3 minutes or until dissolved.

● In food processor, coarsely chop salmon; blend in cream cheese, sour cream and lemon juice until smooth. Add dissolved gelatin; blend until smooth.

● In large bowl, whip cream; fold in all but 1/2 cup (125 mL) of the salmon mixture. Season with salt and pepper to taste. In food processor, blend spinach and remaining salmon mixture until smooth.

● Spread half of the salmon mixture in 9- x 5-inch (2 L) plastic wrap-lined loaf pan. Using back of spoon, carefully spread spinach mixture over top; spread with remaining salmon mixture. Cover with plastic wrap; refrigerate for at least 3 hours or until set. *(Pâté can be refrigerated for up to 24 hours.)* Unmould and serve in slices. Makes about 18 slices.

Use this tasty recipe from food writer Bonnie Stern to make your own version of the popular pastel-pink and forest-green appetizer sold in delis.

Per slice: about
- 136 calories
- 6 g protein
- 12 g fat
- 2 g carbohydrate

Double-Salmon Terrine (left) and Guacamole Pâté with Salsa

Poppy Seed Cheese Roll

Poppy seeds add crunch to a smooth cheese pâté.

Per piece: about
- 55 calories
- 1 g protein
- 5 g fat
- 1 g carbohydrate

8 oz	cream cheese, softened	250 g
1/4 cup	chopped green onions or chives	50 mL
1 tbsp	spicy tomato salsa or ketchup	15 mL
1 tbsp	horseradish	15 mL
Dash	hot pepper sauce	Dash
	Pepper	
2 tbsp	poppy seeds	25 mL

● In bowl, beat together cream cheese, onions, salsa, horseradish, hot pepper sauce, and pepper to taste. Spoon onto plastic wrap and enclose completely. With hands, roll into cylinder about 1-1/2 inches (4 cm) in diameter; refrigerate for 1 hour.

● Unwrap and sprinkle roll evenly with poppy seeds; rewrap and refrigerate for at least 4 hours or for up to 24 hours. Cut into slices to serve. Makes about 18 pieces.

Sun-Dried Tomato Pesto on Brie

A cheese-counter item at Pusateri's, an innovative Toronto specialty food store, inspired this topping for baked Brie. Other alternatives are plain pesto, black olive tapenade, hot pepper jelly and fruit chutney.

Per serving: about
- 150 calories
- 8 g protein
- 12 g fat
- 3 g carbohydrate

1/4 cup	chopped dry-packed sun-dried tomatoes	50 mL
2 tsp	olive oil	10 mL
2	cloves garlic, minced	2
2 tsp	balsamic vinegar	10 mL
1/2 tsp	dried basil	2 mL
1/4 cup	chopped fresh parsley	50 mL
	Pepper	
2	rounds (4 oz/125 g each) Brie cheese	2

● Cover tomatoes with boiling water; let stand for 15 minutes. Drain.

● In small skillet, heat oil over medium heat; cook tomatoes, garlic, vinegar and basil for 1 minute. Remove from heat; stir in parsley, and pepper to taste. Let cool.

● Cut rind off top of each cheese; place cheeses on baking sheet. Top each with tomato mixture. *(Recipe can be prepared to this point, covered and refrigerated for up to 24 hours.)* Bake in 350°F (180°C) oven for 5 to 10 minutes or until cheese melts slightly. Makes 6 servings.

BRIGHTEN YOUR BRIE!

Add an eye-catching touch to a round of Brie: Cut a decorative pattern out of paper the same size as the top of the Brie. Place paper over Brie, dust surface lightly with finely chopped parsley or other herbs, finely chopped toasted pecans, hazelnuts or almonds, or just quickly with paprika. Lift paper and, voilà, a design on the top of the Brie. Stars, hearts, initials, leaves and swirls are all good cutout ideas.

Brie with Cranberry Chutney ▲

1	round (8-inch/20 cm) Brie cheese	1
	Toasted pecan halves (optional)	
	CRANBERRY CHUTNEY	
1 cup	cranberries (fresh or frozen)	250 mL
1/4 cup	packed brown sugar	50 mL
2 tbsp	chopped green onion	25 mL
2 tsp	lime juice	10 mL
1 tsp	chopped pickled jalapeño pepper	5 mL
	Salt and pepper	

● CRANBERRY CHUTNEY: In saucepan, bring cranberries, sugar and 1 tbsp (15 mL) water to boil; reduce heat and simmer, uncovered, for 5 minutes. Add onion, lime juice, jalapeño, and salt and pepper to taste. Let cool slightly. *(Chutney can be covered and refrigerated for up to 3 days.)*

● Place Brie on ovenproof serving dish. Spoon chutney over top. Bake in 350°F (180°C) oven for 10 to 15 minutes or until cheese just starts to melt. Garnish with pecan halves (if using). Makes about 16 servings.

A melty Brie cheese proves irresistible at parties. The cranberry topping is particularly seductive, its tanginess a piquant foil to the rich lushness of Brie.

Per serving: about
- 204 calories
- 12 g protein
- 16 g fat
- 4 g carbohydrate

TIP: Heating Brie on a heatproof serving dish ensures you don't lose any of its ooziness or spoil its looks transferring from baking sheet to plate. Quickly surround with plenty of plain scooping crackers and set out to an appreciative crowd.

Festive Appetizer Cheesecake ◄

1	clove garlic	1
12 oz	cream cheese, softened	375 g
1/3 cup	freshly grated Parmesan cheese	75 mL
2	eggs	2
1 cup	sour cream	250 mL
1/4 cup	minced marinated artichoke hearts	50 mL
1/4 cup	minced oil-packed sun-dried tomatoes	50 mL
	Vegetables and sprouts	
	CRUST	
1/3 cup	butter, softened	75 mL
1	egg yolk	1
1 cup	all-purpose flour	250 mL
1/3 cup	finely chopped pecans	75 mL
1/4 tsp	salt	1 mL

● Lightly grease sides of 12-inch (30 cm) Christmas tree-shaped tart pan with removable bottom or 9-inch (2.5 L) springform pan; line sides with parchment or waxed paper. Center pan on piece of foil; press foil to side of pan right to rim. Place on rimmed baking sheet.

● CRUST: In bowl, mix butter with egg yolk; stir in flour, pecans and salt until crumbly. Press into bottom of pan. Bake in 350°F (180°C) oven for about 30 minutes or until golden. Let cool on sheet on rack.

● Meanwhile, with side of knife, mash garlic on cutting board. In large bowl, beat cream cheese with Parmesan cheese until smooth. Beat in eggs, one at a time; beat in sour cream and garlic. Pour half into separate bowl; stir in artichokes and tomatoes. Spread artichoke mixture over crust. Spread remaining cheese mixture over top.

● Place baking sheet with pan in center of 325°F (160°C) oven; pour in enough hot water to come 1/2 inch (1 cm) up sides of baking sheet. Bake for about 35 minutes or until edges are puffed and center is just set. Let cool on sheet on rack. Cover and refrigerate on sheet for at least 4 hours or until chilled. *(Cheesecake can be refrigerated for up to 2 days.)*

● Remove side of pan and paper. Garnish with vegetables and sprouts. Makes 16 servings.

S*erved with vegetables and crackers, this savory antipasto cheesecake is the stunning star of any party nibbles table. If using a regular springform pan, decorate the cheesecake to suit your occasion.*

Per serving: about
- 213 calories
- 18 g fat
- 5 g protein
- 9 g carbohydrate

Savory Cheddar Cheesecake

1 lb	orange old Cheddar cheese, shredded	500 g
8 oz	cream cheese, softened	250 g
1/2 cup	butter, softened	125 mL
1 tsp	grated orange rind	5 mL
2 tbsp	orange juice	25 mL
1 tbsp	Dijon mustard	15 mL
1/4 tsp	grated nutmeg	1 mL

● In food processor, blend together Cheddar cheese, cream cheese and butter. Add orange rind and juice, mustard and nutmeg; pulse just until combined, thick and creamy.

● Spoon into 8-inch (2 L) plastic wrap-lined springform pan, smoothing top. Cover and refrigerate for at least 8 hours. *(Cheesecake can be refrigerated for up to 3 days.)*

● To serve, remove side of pan; peel off plastic wrap. Transfer to serving plate; let stand for 30 minutes. Makes about 16 servings.

F*rom food writer Jan Main comes this moulded unbaked cheesecake, featuring the nippiness of old Cheddar. Surround with whole wheat biscuits, fresh fruit and a tangy fruit chutney alongside.*

Per serving: about
- 220 calories
- 20 g fat
- good source of calcium
- 8 g protein
- 1 g carbohydrate

Curried Cheesecake Pie ▶

Here's a cracker-bottom pie version of cheesecake that's been given a warm burnish with squash and a whisp of exotica with curry and cumin.

Per serving: about
- 159 calories
- 13 g fat
- 4 g protein
- 7 g carbohydrate

1 cup	finely crushed Ritz crackers	250 mL
3 tbsp	butter, melted	50 mL
	FILLING	
8 oz	cream cheese, softened	250 g
2	eggs	2
1/2 cup	milk	125 mL
1/2 cup	squash purée or puréed carrot	125 mL
1 tsp	curry powder	5 mL
1/2 tsp	salt	2 mL
1/4 tsp	each white pepper and ground cumin	1 mL

● In small bowl, stir cracker crumbs with butter; press evenly over bottom and 1 inch (2.5 cm) up side of 9-inch (23 cm) pie plate, or onto bottom of foil-lined 8-inch (2 L) square cake pan. Bake in 325°F (160°C) oven for 10 minutes. Let cool.

● FILLING: Meanwhile, in bowl or food processor, beat cream cheese until smooth; beat in eggs, one at a time, beating well after each addition. Stir in milk, squash, curry powder, salt, pepper and cumin until blended. Pour over crust.

● Place rimmed baking sheet in center of 325°F (160°C) oven; place pie on baking sheet. Pour enough hot water into baking sheet to come halfway up sides of sheet. Bake for about 30 minutes or until set. Turn oven off. Let cool in water bath in closed oven for 30 minutes. Remove pan from water and let cool completely on rack. Cover and refrigerate for at least 2 hours or until chilled. *(Pie can be refrigerated for up to 2 days.)* Makes 12 servings.

VARIATIONS
● PESTO PARMESAN CHEESE PIE: Omit squash, curry powder, salt, white pepper and cumin; substitute 2 tbsp (25 mL) each pesto and freshly grated Parmesan cheese and 1/4 tsp (1 mL) black pepper. Serve with tomato salsa and black olives.

● TOMATO AND GOAT CHEESE PIE: Omit squash, curry powder, salt and cumin; substitute 1/4 cup (50 mL) cream goat cheese (chèvre) and 2 tbsp (25 mL) finely chopped oil-packed sun-dried tomatoes. Serve on leafy greens garnished with cherry tomatoes.

● SPINACH AND BLUE CHEESE PIE: Omit squash, curry powder and cumin. Reduce salt to 1/4 tsp (1 mL). Substitute 1/2 cup (125 mL) well-drained cooked chopped spinach (about half 10 oz/300 g pkg fresh spinach) and 2 tbsp (25 mL) crumbled blue cheese. Serve with chopped tomato salad.

Herbed Cheese Ball

Cheese balls may sound old hat but their entertaining appeal is eternal. Roll into a ball or pack into a crock.

Per tbsp (15 mL): about
- 52 calories
- 4 g fat
- 3 g protein
- trace carbohydrate

1 lb	old Cheddar cheese, shredded	500 g
4 oz	cream cheese, softened	125 g
1/4 cup	port, brandy or sherry	50 mL
1 tbsp	crumbled dried tarragon, marjoram or oregano	15 mL
Pinch	dried dillweed	Pinch
1/4 cup	chopped fresh parsley	50 mL

● In food processor or bowl, blend together Cheddar cheese, cream cheese, port, tarragon and dillweed until smooth. Shape into ball.

● Spread parsley on waxed paper; roll cheese ball in parsley to coat. Wrap in plastic wrap and refrigerate until chilled. *(Pâté can be refrigerated for up to 2 weeks.)* Makes 1 ball (1-1/4 lb/625 g).

Herbed Yogurt Cheese

3 cups	1% plain yogurt	750 mL
4 tsp	chopped fresh oregano	20 mL
1 tbsp	chopped fresh parsley	15 mL
2 tsp	chopped green onion	10 mL
2 tsp	extra virgin olive oil	10 mL
1/4 tsp	salt	1 mL

● Place yogurt in cheesecloth-lined sieve set over bowl; cover and let drain in refrigerator for 48 hours or until reduced to about 1 cup (250 mL).

● In bowl, stir together drained yogurt, oregano, parsley, onion, oil and salt; mould onto plate with spatula or press into serving bowl. *(Cheese can be covered and refrigerated for up to 24 hours.)* Makes 1 cup (250 mL).

Draining the whey out of yogurt is an ancient method of making cheese and one that Lebanese immigrants to Canada have been using for over 100 years. The spreadable cheese is versatile, taking on any of the herbs, nuts or seeds appropriate to creamy cheese.

TIP: For a firmer cheese, weigh down yogurt with a saucer while draining.

Per tbsp (15 mL): about
- 24 calories
- 1 g fat
- 2 g protein
- 2 g carbohydrate

NINE NIFTY QUICKIES WITH CHEESE

1 Center a block of cream cheese in a shallow dish; spoon chunky fresh or bottled salsa or mango chutney over top and serve with nacho chips or crackers.

2 Place a round of goat cheese (chèvre) in a shallow dish. Sprinkle with chopped fresh rosemary or thyme, drizzle with extra virgin olive oil and surround with black olives (never canned) and water crackers or sliced baguette. For a tongue-tingling version, add some preserved hot red peppers.

3 Serve plump glossy dates or figs with a chunk of Parmesan. It's a blissful combination — a thin shaving of salty cheese atop a sweet dried fruit. Add a few whole salted roasted almonds, pecans or hazelnuts if you like.

4 Serve a block of feta cheese with Greek salad ingredients for nibbling — cherry tomatoes, cucumber slices, black olives — and garnish with fresh oregano.

5 Use herbed cream cheese to fill celery hearts or mushroom caps or to dab on Belgian endive, treviso or radicchio leaves. Garnish with fresh herbs if available.

6 Slice Brie thinly and serve on slices of Jonagold, Mutsu, Golden Delicious or Gala apples or on slices of Bartlett pear. Other good cheese choices include mild Camembert, Fontina or Havarti, trendy Asiago, Grana Padano, Pecorino Romano and blues such as Ermite, Gorgonzola and Stilton.

7 Dab California walnut or pecan halves with cream goat cheese or cream cheese or with cream cheese blended with a bit of Parmesan or the oldest Cheddar you can afford. Top with a second nut half.

8 Cut cream cheese into 3/4-inch (2 cm) cubes; quickly shape into balls. Roll in finely chopped toasted nuts or fresh herbs.

9 Stir chopped fresh herbs such as chives and chervil into spreadable light cream cheese. Garnish top with chive flowers or edible flowers and serve with plain crisp crackers.

Almond Cheeseballs

These crisp and crunchy morsels are at their best served warm and within a few hours of making.

Per piece: about
- 111 calories
- 5 g protein
- 9 g fat
- 3 g carbohydrate

1/2 cup	chopped blanched almonds	125 mL
1/3 cup	crushed unsalted soda crackers	75 mL
1 cup	shredded Swiss cheese	250 mL
1 cup	shredded old Cheddar cheese	250 mL
1/4 cup	all-purpose flour	50 mL
1/4 tsp	each cayenne and black pepper	1 mL
Pinch	salt	Pinch
2	egg whites	2
1/2 cup	vegetable oil	125 mL

● On waxed paper, combine almonds and crackers; set aside.

● In bowl, toss together Swiss cheese, Cheddar cheese, flour, cayenne, black pepper and salt. In separate bowl, beat egg whites until stiff peaks form; fold into cheese mixture.

● Scooping out 1 tbsp (15 mL) at a time, form cheese mixture into balls. Roll each in nut mixture to coat. Cover and refrigerate on plate for at least 1 hour or for up to 24 hours.

● In skillet, heat oil over medium-high heat for 5 minutes; cook balls, in batches and turning often, for 2 to 3 minutes or until golden. With slotted spoon, transfer to paper towels and let drain. Serve warm. *(Cheeseballs can be cooled, covered and refrigerated for up to 4 hours; heat in 400°F/200°C oven for 8 to 10 minutes or until heated through.)* Makes about 18 pieces.

Gorgonzola Pâté

8 oz	Gorgonzola cheese	250 g
4 oz	cream cheese, softened	125 g
1/2 cup	unsalted butter, at room temperature	125 mL
2 tbsp	sour cream	25 mL
1/2 tsp	dried tarragon	2 mL
1/4 tsp	pepper	1 mL
1/2 cup	chopped toasted walnuts	125 mL

● In blender or food processor, blend together Gorgonzola cheese, cream cheese and butter. Stir in sour cream, tarragon and pepper. Stir in nuts. Pack into serving bowl. *(Pâté can be covered and refrigerated for up to 3 days. Let stand at room temperature for 15 to 20 minutes before serving.)* Makes 2-1/2 cups (625 mL).

Garnish a pâté such as this luxurious blue cheese one with whole walnut halves and serve with walnut bread or a crusty Italian sourdough.

Per tbsp (15 mL): about
- 65 calories
- 6 g fat
- 2 g protein
- 1 g carbohydrate

Huron County Cheese Log

8 oz	old Cheddar cheese, shredded	250 g
1/2 cup	crushed salted soda crackers	125 mL
1	hard-cooked egg, chopped	1
1/3 cup	finely chopped sweet pickle	75 mL
1/3 cup	minced green onions	75 mL
1/3 cup	mayonnaise	75 mL
3 tbsp	finely chopped sweet green pepper	50 mL
2 tbsp	chopped pimiento	25 mL
1 tbsp	chopped stuffed olives	15 mL

● In large bowl, combine cheese, crackers, egg, pickle, onions, mayonnaise, green pepper, pimiento and olives. Using hands or wooden spoon, mash until well combined and holding together.

● Form mixture into 12-inch (30 cm) long log. Wrap in waxed paper and refrigerate for about 1 hour or until firm. *(Log can be refrigerated for up to 2 days.)* Cut into slices to serve. Makes about 12 pieces.

From the Armstrongs of Stanley Township in southwestern Ontario comes a family reunion favorite that originated in a local home economics class.

Per piece: about
- 149 calories
- 12 g fat
- 6 g protein
- 5 g carbohydrate

(From bottom left) Huron County Cheese Log, Very Red Pepper Dip (p. 43), a platter of crudités, Feta-Stuffed Cherry Tomatoes (p. 78)

Dips and Spreads

Help-yourself dips and spreads encourage sharing. That buzz around the bowl invites friendliness and conversation and provides a relaxed prelude to a meal. From traditional to trendy, here are tasty bowlfuls of the best to enhance any occasion.

Creamy Hummus ▶

A delicious classic dip from Greece and the Middle East, hummus has become thoroughly mainstream. Be sure to stir the water into the dip after processing or it will simply be absorbed and not make the dip creamy.

Per tbsp (15 mL): about
- 38 calories
- 3 g fat
- 1 g protein
- 2 g carbohydrate

1	can (19 oz/540 mL) chick-peas, drained and rinsed	1
1/2 cup	tahini	125 mL
1/3 cup	olive oil	75 mL
1/3 cup	lemon juice	75 mL
1/2 tsp	ground coriander	2 mL
1/4 tsp	ground cumin	1 mL
2	large cloves garlic, minced	2
3 tbsp	chopped fresh parsley	50 mL
	Salt and pepper	

● In food processor, purée together chick-peas, tahini, oil, lemon juice, coriander and cumin until smooth; transfer to bowl.

● Stir in garlic, parsley and 1/4 cup (50 mL) water. Season with salt and pepper to taste. Makes 3 cups (750 mL).

Minted Tzatziki ▶

For the best tzatziki, choose a yogurt made without gelatin. You can drain the cucumber ahead of time, but don't stir it into the yogurt mixture until just ready to serve.

Per tbsp (15 mL): about
- 19 calories
- 1 g fat
- 1 g protein
- 1 g carbohydrate

2 cups	plain yogurt	500 mL
Half	English cucumber	Half
1/2 tsp	salt	2 mL
2 tbsp	chopped fresh mint	25 mL
1 tbsp	each olive oil and lemon juice	15 mL
3	cloves garlic, minced	3
1/4 tsp	pepper	1 mL

● Place yogurt in cheesecloth-lined sieve set over bowl; cover and let drain in refrigerator for at least 3 hours or for up to 24 hours or until reduced to 1 cup (250 mL).

● Peel and grate cucumber into another sieve; sprinkle with half of the salt. Let drain for 1 hour.

● In bowl, stir together drained yogurt and cucumber, remaining salt, mint, oil, lemon juice, garlic and pepper. Makes 1-1/2 cups (375 mL).

(Clockwise from left) Creamy Hummus, Grilled Eggplant Dip (p. 40) and Minted Tzatziki

Grilled Eggplant Dip

The smokiness of grilled eggplant does add a magical extra to this Greek dip — but when the grilling's chilly, roast the eggplant in the oven on a heavy baking sheet (photo, p. 39).

Per tbsp (15 mL): about
- 14 calories
- 1 g fat
- trace protein
- 2 g carbohydrate

2	eggplants (about 2 lb/1 kg)	2
2	cloves garlic, minced	2
1	green onion, minced	1
2 tbsp	chopped fresh parsley	25 mL
2 tbsp	olive oil	25 mL
1 tbsp	chopped fresh basil	15 mL
1 tbsp	lemon juice	15 mL
1 tsp	Dijon mustard	5 mL
	Salt and pepper	

● With fork, prick eggplants. Place on greased grill over medium-high heat; close lid and cook, turning occasionally, for 45 to 50 minutes or until tender and charred all over. Let stand on plate until cool enough to handle, reserving juices.

● Cut eggplants in half lengthwise. With spoon, scoop out flesh into food processor or bowl, adding any juices from plate; purée or mash with fork. Transfer to bowl.

● Stir in garlic, onion, parsley, oil, basil, lemon juice and mustard. Season with salt and pepper to taste. Makes 2 cups (500 mL).

Asian Veggie Dip

When you're looking for a taste partner for your favorite green vegetable, this is the dip for you.

Per tbsp (15 mL): about
- 50 calories
- 5 g fat
- 0 g protein
- 2 g carbohydrate

2 cups	light mayonnaise	500 mL
2 tbsp	rice vinegar	25 mL
1 tbsp	sesame oil	15 mL
2 tsp	orange juice	10 mL
1 tsp	granulated sugar	5 mL
1 tsp	soy sauce	5 mL
2 tsp	grated gingerroot	10 mL
1 tsp	grated orange rind	5 mL
	Toasted sesame seeds (optional)	

● In small bowl, whisk together mayonnaise, vinegar, oil, orange juice, sugar and soy sauce until blended. Stir in ginger and orange rind. Sprinkle with sesame seeds (if using). Makes 2 cups (500 mL).

YOUR OWN CRISP DIPPERS

MELBA TOAST
● Thinly slice bread and arrange in single layer on baking sheets. Toast in 350°F (180°C) oven until golden and crisp, about 40 minutes.

BAGEL CRISPS
● Using sharp serrated knife, cut 4 bagels in half to make 2 semicircles; slice horizontally into 1/8-inch (3 mm) thick slices. Place in single layer on ungreased baking sheets.
● Brush both sides with 1/3 cup (75 mL) vegetable oil (approx); sprinkle lightly with salt. Bake in 400°F (200°C) oven for about 12 minutes or until crisp and light golden. Makes about 36 pieces.

GRILLED PITAS
● In small bowl, whisk together 2 tbsp (25 mL) olive oil, 1/2 tsp (2 mL) paprika, and 1/4 tsp (1 mL) cayenne pepper (optional); evenly brush half over 1 side of each of four 8-inch (20 cm) pitas. Place, oiled side down, on greased grill over medium heat; close lid and cook for 2 minutes.
● Brush with remaining oil mixture; turn and cook for about 2 minutes longer or until pitas are crisp and grill-marked. Cut into wedges or tear into pieces. Makes about 32 pieces.

Banana Curry Dip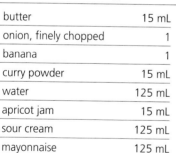

1 tbsp	butter	15 mL
1	onion, finely chopped	1
1	banana	1
1 tbsp	curry powder	15 mL
1/2 cup	water	125 mL
1 tbsp	apricot jam	15 mL
1/2 cup	sour cream	125 mL
1/2 cup	mayonnaise	125 mL
1/2 tsp	salt	2 mL
	Pepper	

● In saucepan, melt butter over medium heat; cook onion, stirring occasionally, for 3 minutes or until softened but not browned. Push to side of pan.

● Thickly slice banana; add to pan and cook for 1 minute. Add curry powder; cook for 1 minute, stirring to combine.

● Add water and bring to boil; reduce heat and simmer for 10 minutes or until thickened and liquid is reduced by half. Remove from heat; stir in jam.

● Transfer to food processor or blender; purée until smooth. Add sour cream, mayonnaise, salt, and pepper to taste; mix just until combined. Transfer to bowl. *(Dip can be covered and refrigerated for up to 24 hours; let stand at room temperature for 30 minutes.)* Makes 2 cups (500 mL).

*Y*ou may need to be convinced to try this fruit-based dip, but be assured that it is positively terrific, not only with crunchy vegetables but also with crackers, chicken fingers and wings.

Per tbsp (15 mL): about
● 41 calories
● 4 g fat
● trace protein
● 2 g carbohydrate

Herbed Crab Quickie ▲

It's worth keeping a can of crab in your cupboard to be able to make this impressive dip at a moment's notice.

Per tbsp (15 mL): about
- 17 calories
- 1 g fat
- 2 g protein
- 1 g carbohydrate

1/2 cup	1% plain yogurt	125 mL
1	can (6 oz/170 g) crabmeat, well drained	1
1/4 cup	light mayonnaise	50 mL
1 tbsp	chopped fresh dill	15 mL
1 tsp	lemon juice	5 mL
1/4 tsp	pepper	1 mL
Dash	hot pepper sauce	Dash

● In small bowl, combine yogurt, crabmeat, mayonnaise, dill, lemon juice, pepper and hot pepper sauce. *(Dip can be covered and refrigerated for up to 24 hours.)* Makes 1-1/4 cups (300 mL).

Very Red Pepper Dip

3/4 cup	chopped roasted red pepper	175 mL
1/2 cup	light mayonnaise	125 mL
2 tbsp	light sour cream	25 mL
2 tsp	red wine vinegar	10 mL
Pinch	granulated sugar	Pinch
1 tbsp	chopped fresh oregano	15 mL
1/4 tsp	chopped fresh rosemary (optional)	1 mL

● In food processor, purée together red pepper, mayonnaise, sour cream, vinegar and sugar until smooth. Transfer to small bowl. Stir in oregano, and rosemary (if using). *(Dip can be covered and refrigerated for up to 24 hours.)* Makes 1-1/4 cups (300 mL).

*O*ut-of-season red peppers *are expensive but roasted ones are available in jars. You will need one lovely big sweet red bell pepper for this colorful appetizer (photo, p. 37).*

Per tbsp (15 mL): about
- 21 calories
- 2 g fat
- trace protein
- 1 g carbohydrate

TIP: To roast red pepper, broil or grill 1 sweet red pepper, turning several times, for 20 minutes or until blistered and charred. Let cool; peel, core, seed and chop to make 3/4 cup (175 mL).

Artichoke Dip in a Snap

1	jar (6 oz/170 mL) marinated artichoke hearts	1
4 oz	light cream cheese, softened	125 g
2 tbsp	light sour cream	25 mL
1 tbsp	vegetable oil	15 mL
1/2 tsp	dry mustard	2 mL
Pinch	pepper	Pinch
1/4 cup	chopped fresh basil	50 mL

● Drain artichoke hearts. In food processor, purée together artichoke hearts, cream cheese, sour cream, oil, mustard and pepper until smooth. Transfer to small bowl. *(Dip can be covered and refrigerated for up to 24 hours.)* Stir in basil. Makes 1 cup (250 mL).

*T*hank goodness for food *processors. With one ready on the counter, you can greet guests with this dip in just minutes.*

Per tbsp (15 mL): about
- 22 calories
- 2 g fat
- 1 g protein
- 1 g carbohydrate

Fresh Beet and Onion Dip

1/2 cup	quark cheese or light sour cream or light cream cheese	125 mL
1/2 cup	2% plain yogurt	125 mL
1/4 cup	shredded raw beet	50 mL
2	green onions, finely chopped	2
2 tsp	lemon juice	10 mL
1/4 tsp	each salt, pepper and granulated sugar	1 mL

● In small bowl, mix together quark, yogurt, beet, onions, lemon juice, salt, pepper and sugar. *(Dip can be covered and refrigerated for up to 8 hours.)* Makes 1-1/4 cups (300 mL).

*O*ur nutrition editor, Anne *Lindsay, created this lightened-up, strikingly pink dip that's sure to be a conversation piece around a buffet table. After just one mouthful, guests will be hooked on its great taste.*

Per tbsp (15 mL): about
- 11 calories
- 1 g fat
- 1 g protein
- 1 g carbohydrate

TIP: Quark is much lower in fat than many cheeses. It's also milder than low-fat yogurt but has a richer texture. Use it in dips, sauces and cheesecakes.

Creamy Chèvre Dip

Goat cheese (chèvre) has more oomph than regular cream cheese but either one can be used for this easy crowd-pleaser.

Per tbsp (15 mL): about
• 32 calories   • 1 g protein
• 3 g fat   • 1 g carbohydrate

6 oz	cream goat cheese (chèvre)	175 g
1-1/2 cups	sour cream	375 mL
1	clove garlic, minced	1
1/2 tsp	each crumbled dried rosemary and thyme	2 mL
Dash	hot pepper sauce	Dash
3 tbsp	chopped oil-packed sun-dried tomatoes	50 mL
2 tbsp	chopped fresh parsley	25 mL
2	green onions, chopped	2

● In food processor or bowl, beat together goat cheese, sour cream, garlic, rosemary, thyme and hot pepper sauce until smooth.

● Stir in tomatoes, parsley and green onions. Transfer to small bowl. *(Dip can be covered and refrigerated for up to 2 days; serve at room temperature.)* Makes about 2 cups (500 mL).

Caesar Tofu Dip ▶

Want to add tofu to your diet? You need maxi flavor from other ingredients to succeed, as our Test Kitchen did with this luscious dip. The Caesar flavors are particularly delicious paired with hearts of romaine or with Belgian endive.

Per tbsp (15 mL): about
• 20 calories   • 1 g protein
• 2 g fat   • 1 g carbohydrate

1 cup	tofu	250 mL
2 tbsp	light mayonnaise	25 mL
2 tbsp	plain yogurt	25 mL
1 tbsp	lemon juice	15 mL
2 tsp	Worcestershire sauce	10 mL
1 tsp	Dijon mustard	5 mL
1 tsp	anchovy paste	5 mL
Dash	hot pepper sauce	Dash
1/4 cup	freshly grated Parmesan cheese	50 mL
1	clove garlic, minced	1
1 tsp	olive oil	5 mL
	Salt and pepper	

● In food processor, purée together tofu, mayonnaise, yogurt, lemon juice, Worcestershire sauce, mustard, anchovy paste and hot pepper sauce until smooth. Transfer to small bowl.

● Stir in Parmesan cheese, garlic and oil; season with salt and pepper to taste. *(Dip can be covered and refrigerated for up to 8 hours.)* Makes 1-1/3 cups (325 mL).

Spicy Bean Dip

As far as dips are concerned, beans have what it takes for texture. But to match in the flavor department, they need some freshness from lemon and the aromatics of cumin.

Per tbsp (15 mL): about
• 20 calories   • 1 g protein
• trace fat   • 4 g carbohydrate

1	can (19 oz/540 mL) white kidney beans, drained and rinsed	1
3 tbsp	lemon juice	50 mL
1-1/2 tsp	ground cumin	7 mL
2	cloves garlic, minced	2
1/2 tsp	pepper	2 mL
2	green onions, chopped	2

● In food processor, purée together beans, lemon juice, cumin, garlic and pepper. Transfer to small bowl. Cover and refrigerate for at least 1 hour. *(Dip can be refrigerated for up to 2 days.)* Sprinkle with green onions. Makes about 1-1/2 cups (375 mL).

(In bowl) Caesar Tofu Dip (p. 44); (on tray) Barbecued Salmon Spread on bread, Mini Crab Quiches (p. 54)

Barbecued Salmon Spread ▲

8 oz	light cream cheese	250 g
6 oz	chopped skinless barbecued salmon bits or smoked salmon	175 g
1/3 cup	chopped fresh dill	75 mL

● In bowl, beat cream cheese until creamy. Beat in salmon and dill until well mixed. Transfer to small bowl. *(Spread can be covered and refrigerated for up to 2 days.)* Makes about 1-3/4 cups (425 mL).

P*acify ravenous appetites with a spread that hails from the West Coast.*

Per tbsp (15 mL): about
- 29 calories
- 2 g fat
- 2 g protein
- 1 g carbohydrate

Blue Cheese and Walnut Spread

This blend of blue cheese and walnuts is a sure way to please guests at both casual and dress-up events. Serve with whole wheat digestive crackers for that satisfying sweet and salty combo.

Per tbsp (15 mL): about
- 84 calories
- 8 g fat
- 3 g protein
- 1 g carbohydrate

4 oz	Gorgonzola or other creamy blue cheese	125 g
4 oz	cream cheese, softened	125 g
1/2 cup	coarsely chopped walnuts	125 mL
2 tbsp	brandy	25 mL
	Pepper	
	Walnut halves	

● In bowl or food processor, beat Gorgonzola cheese with cream cheese until smooth, being careful not to overmix.

● Fold in chopped walnuts, brandy, and pepper to taste. Transfer to small bowl, smoothing top; garnish with walnut halves. *(Spread can be covered and refrigerated for up to 10 days.)* Makes about 1 cup (250 mL).

TIP: For a tasty dip, blend in 1 cup (250 mL) sour cream along with the cheese.

Feta and Ricotta Spread

A mild creamy cheese such as ricotta or light cream cheese smooths out the craggy peaks of assertive feta. Keep the easy steps in mind and vary to suit your tastes and whatever you have in the fridge.

Per tbsp (15 mL): about
- 36 calories
- 3 g fat
- 2 g protein
- 1 g carbohydrate

8 oz	feta cheese	250 g
8 oz	ricotta cheese	250 g
1 tbsp	lemon juice	15 mL
1 tbsp	olive oil	15 mL
2	cloves garlic, minced	2
1 tsp	dried oregano or mint	5 mL
2 tbsp	plain yogurt (approx)	25 mL

● Crumble feta cheese into small bowl; mash in ricotta, lemon juice and oil until almost smooth. Stir in garlic and oregano. Blend in enough of the yogurt until of spreading consistency. Cover and refrigerate for at least 2 hours or until thickened slightly. *(Spread can be refrigerated for up to 2 days.)* Makes about 2 cups (500 mL).

TIP: Feta cheeses vary widely in firmness and saltiness; for this recipe, choose a fairly soft, mild feta (usually made from sheep's milk) rather than a drier saltier variety.

Provençale Tuna Spread

Top sliced French bread, or use this spread by food writer Bonnie Stern as a filling for party sandwiches (see p. 16).

Per tbsp (15 mL): about
- 41 calories
- 3 g fat
- 2 g protein
- trace carbohydrate

1	can (6-1/2 oz/184 g) flaked white tuna	1
8 oz	cream cheese, softened	250 g
1	clove garlic, minced	1
2	anchovy fillets, minced (or 2 tsp/10 mL anchovy paste)	2
2 tbsp	lemon juice	25 mL
1/2 tsp	pepper	2 mL
1/4 cup	chopped black olives	50 mL
2 tbsp	chopped fresh parsley	25 mL

● In food processor, purée together tuna, cream cheese, garlic, anchovy fillets, lemon juice and pepper until smooth; stir in olives and parsley. Transfer to small bowl. *(Spread can be covered and refrigerated for up to 24 hours.)* Makes 2 cups (500 mL).

Marinated Herring and Apple Spread

6 oz	cream cheese, softened	175 g
1/4 cup	sour cream	50 mL
2/3 cup	finely chopped marinated herring	150 mL
2/3 cup	finely chopped (unpeeled) red apple	150 mL
2 tbsp	chopped pickled onion	25 mL
	Pepper	

● In bowl, blend cream cheese with sour cream. Mix in marinated herring, apple, pickled onion, and pepper to taste. Transfer to small bowl. *(Spread can be covered and refrigerated for up to 3 days.)* Makes about 1-3/4 cups (425 mL).

Try this chunky fresh-tasting dip on rye crackers or Scandinavian flatbread.

Per tbsp (15 mL): about
- 45 calories
- 2 g protein
- 4 g fat
- 1 g carbohydrate

TIP: You can find jars of herring tidbits pickled with onions in delis and supermarkets. Drain, reserving herrings and onions for the spread.

A TRIO OF BREAD SPREADS

Set out matching bowls of these spreads for a help-yourself party. Cocktail pumpernickel or rye bread rounds (about 1-1/2 inches/4 cm in diameter) are perfect for these toppings. Or use melba toast rounds or water crackers, or cut rounds out of bread slices with a sharp cookie cutter and toast.

SMOKED SALMON HORSERADISH BUTTER ROUNDS

1/3 cup	butter, at room temperature	75 mL
2 tbsp	cream cheese, softened	25 mL
1 tbsp	horseradish	15 mL
Pinch	pepper	Pinch
48	cocktail pumpernickel rounds	48
4 oz	smoked salmon, cut in strips	125 g
	Dill sprigs	

● In bowl, beat together butter, cream cheese, horseradish and pepper until smooth. Cover and refrigerate for at least 12 hours. *(Spread can be refrigerated for up to 3 days.)* Spread on bread; top each with salmon. Garnish with dill. Makes 48 pieces.

Per piece: about • 53 calories • 2 g protein
• 2 g fat • 8 g carbohydrate

GOAT CHEESE AND SUN-DRIED TOMATO ROUNDS

1/4 cup	dry-packed sun-dried tomatoes	50 mL
8 oz	cream goat cheese (chèvre)	250 g
1/4 cup	chopped fresh parsley	50 mL
3 tbsp	18% cream	50 mL
1/2 tsp	grated lemon rind	2 mL
48	melba toast or water crackers	48
	Black olive slices	

● Pour boiling water over tomatoes; let stand for 10 minutes. Drain and finely chop. In small bowl, mix together cheese, parsley, cream, lemon rind and tomatoes. *(Spread can be covered and refrigerated for up to 24 hours.)* Spread on toast rounds; garnish each with olive slice. Makes 48 pieces.

Per piece: about • 25 calories • 1 g protein
• 1 g fat • 2 g carbohydrate

BRANDIED APRICOT CHEESE ROUNDS

8 oz	cream cheese, softened	250 g
2 tbsp	brandy	25 mL
1/3 cup	finely chopped dried apricots	75 mL
48	cocktail pumpernickel rounds	48
48	toasted walnut halves	48

● In bowl, beat cream cheese with brandy until smooth. Stir in apricots. *(Spread can be covered and refrigerated for up to 5 days.)* Spread on bread; garnish each with walnut. Makes 48 pieces.

Per piece: about • 71 calories • 2 g protein
• 3 g fat • 9 g carbohydrate

Pastry Pleasers

Revel in the tantalizing nibbles that come tucked into golden, crisp pastry. With easy-to-handle and freezer-available phyllo, puff and short pastry, all kinds of these impressive tidbits are just waiting to be tried.

Smoked Salmon Palmiers ▶

Pastry needs strong, distinctive flavors to balance its richness. Smoked salmon qualifies beautifully and makes an attractive swirl, too.

Per piece: about
- 105 calories
- 8 g fat
- 2 g protein
- 6 g carbohydrate

1/2 cup	cream cheese, softened	125 mL
2 oz	smoked salmon, finely chopped (about 3 tbsp/50 mL)	60 g
1 tbsp	chopped fresh dill	15 mL
Pinch	pepper	Pinch
1 lb	Quick Puff Pastry (recipe, p. 50)	500 g
1	egg, beaten	1

● In bowl, beat cream cheese until fluffy; stir in salmon, dill and pepper until combined. Set aside.

● On well-floured surface, roll out pastry into 16- x 12-inch (40 x 30 cm) rectangle. Spread with salmon mixture, leaving 1/2-inch (1 cm) border on all sides. Brush border with some of the egg.

● Starting at long side, roll up jelly roll-style just to center of rectangle; roll up other side to meet in center. Using serrated knife, cut in half crosswise. Transfer to baking sheet; cover and refrigerate for about 30 minutes or until firm.

● Brush all over with egg; transfer to cutting board. Using serrated knife, trim ends; cut into 1/2-inch (1 cm) thick slices. Place, cut side up, on lightly greased or parchment paper-lined baking sheets. Cover and refrigerate for at least 1 hour or for up to 8 hours. *(Palmiers can be frozen in single layers and stored in rigid airtight container for up to 1 week; do not thaw.)*

● Bake in center of 425°F (220°C) oven for 14 to 18 minutes or until puffed and golden. Makes about 28 pieces.

PUFF PASTRY APPETIZERS

While our Quick Puff Pastry (recipe, p. 50) is especially tasty, you can also substitute store-bought when making the puff pastry appetizers in this chapter. It is available in packages slightly smaller than 1 lb (500 g), so the recipe yield will be slightly smaller.

(Clockwise from top) Smoked Salmon Palmier; Flaky Diamond (p. 51); Pesto Crescent (p. 51); Bite-Size Curried Shrimp Tart (p. 50); and puff pastry shapes in stars, moon and snowman (see box, p. 50).

Bite-Size Curried Shrimp Tarts ▼

A special occasion is what you need to make these sophisticated tartlets.

Per piece: about
• 110 calories   • 2 g protein
• 8 g fat   • 9 g carbohydrate

1 lb	Quick Puff Pastry (recipe, this page)	500 g
1	can (4 oz/113 g) cocktail shrimp	1
1/3 cup	mango chutney, chunks removed	75 mL
1/2 tsp	curry powder	2 mL

● Cut pastry in half; wrap one piece and set aside in refrigerator.

● On well-floured surface, roll out remaining pastry to 1/4-inch (5 mm) thickness. Using 2-1/4-inch (5.5 cm) round crinkle cookie cutter, cut out 12 circles. Fit into 1-3/4-inch (4.5 cm) tart cups, pressing down edges gently. Refrigerate for about 30 minutes or until firm. Repeat with remaining pastry.

● Meanwhile, drain and pat shrimp dry; transfer to bowl. Add chutney and curry powder; mix well. Divide evenly among chilled tart shells.

● Bake in center of 450°F (230°C) oven for 14 to 18 minutes or until puffed and golden. Makes 24 pieces.

QUICK PUFF PASTRY

You can make an array of delectable party appetizers from this surprisingly easy dough. Follow instructions carefully, especially times for processing; overprocessing produces paste.

1 cup	cold unsalted butter	250 mL
1-2/3 cups	all-purpose flour	400 mL
3/4 tsp	salt	4 mL
1/3 cup	cold water	75 mL

● Cut butter into 1/2-inch (1 cm) cubes; set aside 3/4 cup (175 mL) in refrigerator. In food processor, blend flour with salt; sprinkle with remaining butter. Using on/off motion, cut in butter for about 30 seconds or until in small pieces indistinguishable from flour.

● Sprinkle with reserved chilled butter; pulse twice to break into smaller pieces. Pour water evenly over mixture (not through feed tube); pulse 3 or 4 times or just until mixture is loose and ragged-looking.

● Transfer to lightly floured surface; gather together and knead lightly. Press into rectangle; place on floured pastry cloth or waxed paper. With stockinette-covered rolling pin, roll out to 15- x 12-inch (38 x 30 cm) rectangle.

● Starting at one long edge, fold over one-third; fold other long edge over top, flush with first fold, to make 15- x 4-inch (38 x 10 cm) rectangle. Starting from one of the short ends, roll up jelly roll-style, tucking in rolled-up edges. Press into square. Wrap in plastic wrap and refrigerate for about 1 hour or until firm. *(Pastry can be refrigerated for up to 5 days or frozen in freezer bag for up to 2 weeks.)* Makes 1 lb (500 g) pastry.

To make puff pastry shapes
● On well-floured surface, roll out 1 lb (500 g) puff pastry to 1/4-inch (5 mm) thickness. Using 2-1/2-inch (6 cm) cookie cutters, cut out shapes; place on lightly greased or parchment paper-lined baking sheets. Whisk 1 egg with 1 tbsp (50 mL) water; brush over shapes. Sprinkle with 1/4 cup (25 mL) sesame or poppy seeds. Cover and refrigerate for about 15 minutes or until firm. Bake in center of 425°F (220°C) oven for 10 to 15 minutes or until shapes are puffed and golden. Makes 25 pieces.

TIP: For easy rolling out of pastry, use a pastry cloth and stockinette-covered rolling pin dusted with flour. If you don't have these, roll out pastry on well-floured work surface or between sheets of flour-dusted waxed paper.

Flaky Diamonds

1	can (3.67 oz/104 g) smoked oysters, drained	1
1 lb	Quick Puff Pastry (recipe, p. 50)	500 g
1	egg	1

● Cut each oyster in half crosswise; drain on paper towel to soak up excess oil.

● On well-floured surface, roll out pastry into 18- x 12-inch (45 x 30 cm) rectangle. Cut lengthwise into 1-1/2-inch (4 cm) wide strips. Cut crosswise diagonally into 2-1/2-inch (6 cm) widths to make diamonds.

● Whisk egg with 1 tbsp (15 mL) water. Place half an oyster in center of half of the diamonds; brush pastry around oyster with some of the egg mixture. Top with plain diamond, matching shapes to form sandwich; press edges to seal. Place on lightly greased or parchment paper-lined baking sheets; crimp edges with fork.

● Brush tops with remaining egg mixture. Cover and refrigerate for about 30 minutes or until firm. *(Diamonds can be refrigerated for up to 8 hours or frozen in single layers and stored in rigid airtight containers for up to 1 week; do not thaw.)*

● Bake in center of 425°F (220°C) oven for 10 to 15 minutes or until puffed and golden. Makes 30 pieces.

VARIATIONS
● ANCHOVY DIAMONDS: Substitute 1 can (50 g) anchovies for oysters; cut each into 1-inch (2.5 cm) pieces.

● SUN-DRIED TOMATO DIAMONDS: Substitute 8 dry-packed sun-dried tomatoes for oysters. Quarter and soak in boiling water for 20 minutes; drain.

Smoked oysters, sun-dried tomatoes and anchovies are just some of the intense flavors that match well with puff pastry (photo, p. 49).

Per piece: about
- 85 calories
- 7 g fat
- 1 g protein
- 6 g carbohydrate

Pesto Crescents ▼

1 lb	Quick Puff Pastry (recipe, p. 50)	500 g
1/2 cup	pesto	125 mL
1	egg, beaten	1

● Cut pastry in half; wrap one piece and set aside in refrigerator.

● On well-floured surface, roll out remaining pastry into 12- x 8-inch (30 x 20 cm) rectangle. Cut in half lengthwise. Cut each piece crosswise into four 3-inch (8 cm) widths; cut each in half diagonally.

● Spread each triangle with about 1/2 tsp (2 mL) pesto, leaving 1/2 inch (1 cm) uncovered at top point. Brush uncovered point with egg. Starting at bottom, roll up jelly roll-style and shape into crescents, pressing at point to seal.

● Place on lightly greased or parchment paper-lined baking sheets; brush with egg. Repeat with remaining pastry. Cover and refrigerate for at least 30 minutes or for up to 8 hours. *(Crescents can be frozen in single layers and stored in rigid airtight containers for up to 1 week; do not thaw.)*

● Bake in center of 425°F (220°C) oven for 14 to 18 minutes or until puffed and golden. Makes 32 pieces.

Homemade pesto, frozen in small amounts, comes in very handy when it's time to make appetizers. Bought pesto is just as good, but pricey.

Per piece: about
- 90 calories
- 8 g fat
- 1 g protein
- 5 g carbohydrate

Ham and Cheese Squares

For entertaining ease, these popular savory squares can be made a day ahead.

Per piece: about
- 58 calories
- 4 g protein
- 4 g fat
- 2 g carbohydrate

1	pkg (10 oz/284 g) fresh spinach, trimmed	1
2	eggs	2
1	pkg (411 g) frozen puff pastry, thawed	1
2 tbsp	Dijon mustard	25 mL
1-1/4 lb	thinly sliced cooked ham	625 g
12 oz	sliced Swiss cheese	375 g
1 tsp	(approx) milk	5 mL

● Rinse spinach; shake off excess water. In large pot, cover and cook spinach over medium heat, with just the water clinging to leaves, for about 2 minutes or just until wilted. Drain and squeeze dry; chop and set aside.

● Separate 1 of the eggs; set yolk aside for glaze. Whisk white with whole egg; set aside.

● On lightly floured surface, roll out half of the pastry and fit into 17- x 11-inch (45 x 29 cm) jelly roll pan or rimmed baking sheet. Spread with mustard, leaving 1-inch (2.5 cm) border uncovered. Top with half of the ham and half of the cheese. Top with spinach; drizzle with egg white mixture. Top with remaining ham and cheese. Fold pastry border up around filling. Beat reserved yolk with milk; brush edges of pastry with some of the glaze. Cover and refrigerate remaining glaze.

● Roll out remaining pastry and fit over top, pressing edges with floured fork to seal. Cover with plastic wrap and refrigerate for at least 1 hour or for up to 24 hours.

● Brush with some of the remaining glaze; let stand in refrigerator for about 30 minutes. Brush with remaining glaze, adding a bit more milk if not enough glaze. Score pastry into bite-size squares; slash 2 or 3 steam vents in top. Bake in center of 425°F (220°C) oven for about 20 minutes or until puffed and golden brown. Let stand for 10 minutes before cutting into squares. Makes about 72 pieces.

Prosciutto Scrolls ▶

Rolled in from both ends like a scroll, this puff pastry treat can be assembled and waiting in the fridge for last-minute baking to crisp, golden perfection.

Per piece: about
- 64 calories
- 2 g protein
- 4 g fat
- 5 g carbohydrate

1	pkg (411 g) frozen puff pastry, thawed	1
2 tbsp	sweet mustard	25 mL
1/4 cup	freshly grated Parmesan cheese	50 mL
4 oz	thinly sliced prosciutto (or 6 oz/175 g sliced smoked ham)	125 g
1	egg, beaten	1

● On lightly floured surface, roll out half of the pastry into 12- x 10-inch (30 x 25 cm) rectangle. Spread with half of the mustard, leaving 1/2-inch (1 cm) border uncovered. Sprinkle with half of the cheese; arrange half of the prosciutto in single layer over cheese. Brush border with water.

● Starting at short side, roll up jelly roll-style just to center of rectangle; roll up other side to meet in center. Gently turn over. Using serrated knife, trim ends; cut into 1/2-inch (1 cm) thick slices. Place, cut side down, on parchment paper-lined baking sheets; press lightly. Repeat with remaining pastry. Cover and refrigerate for 1 hour. *(Scrolls can be prepared to this point and refrigerated for up to 24 hours.)*

● Brush with egg. Bake in center of 400°F (200°C) oven for 15 to 18 minutes or until puffed and lightly golden. Makes about 34 pieces.

(Clockwise from top left) snow peas piped with cream cheese, Prosciutto Scrolls, Asian Meatballs (p. 88), Almond Cheeseballs (p. 36); (in center) Christmas Quiche Wedges, Savory Phyllo Cups (p. 58)

Christmas Quiche Wedges ▼

1-2/3 cups	all-purpose flour	400 mL
Pinch	salt	Pinch
1/2 cup	cold butter	125 mL
1/4 cup	cold water	50 mL
1	egg yolk	1
1 tbsp	vegetable oil	15 mL
	FILLING	
1/3 cup	shredded mozzarella cheese	75 mL
1/2 cup	each thinly sliced sweet green and red pepper	125 mL
2	eggs	2
1 cup	milk or 18% cream	250 mL
1/2 tsp	each dried oregano and salt	2 mL
1/4 tsp	pepper	1 mL

● In bowl, combine flour and salt; with pastry blender or two knives, cut in butter until mixture resembles fine crumbs with a few larger pieces. Beat together water, egg yolk and oil; stir into flour mixture until moistened. Turn out onto lightly floured surface; knead into ball. Wrap in plastic wrap and refrigerate for at least 1 hour or for up to 5 days.

● On lightly floured surface, roll out pastry to 1/8-inch (3 mm) thickness; cut out five 6-inch (15 cm) rounds. Fit each into 4-inch (10 cm) quiche or tart pan with removable bottom. Refrigerate for 30 minutes.

● Line each shell with foil; weigh down with pie weights or dried beans. Bake on baking sheet in center of 375°F (190°C) oven for 15 minutes; remove weights and foil. Prick pastry with fork; bake for 10 minutes longer or until golden brown. *(Shells can be cooled, covered and stored at room temperature for up to 1 day.)*

● FILLING: Divide mozzarella evenly among shells; top with green and red peppers. In bowl, whisk eggs; whisk in milk, oregano, salt and pepper. Pour into shells.

● Bake for 35 to 40 minutes or until knife inserted in centers comes out clean. Let cool on rack for 10 minutes; cut each tart into 6 wedges. Makes 30 pieces.

Sweet red and green pepper strips are all you need to turn custardy quiche into festive holiday fare.

Per piece: about
- 73 calories
- 5 g fat
- 2 g protein
- 6 g carbohydrate

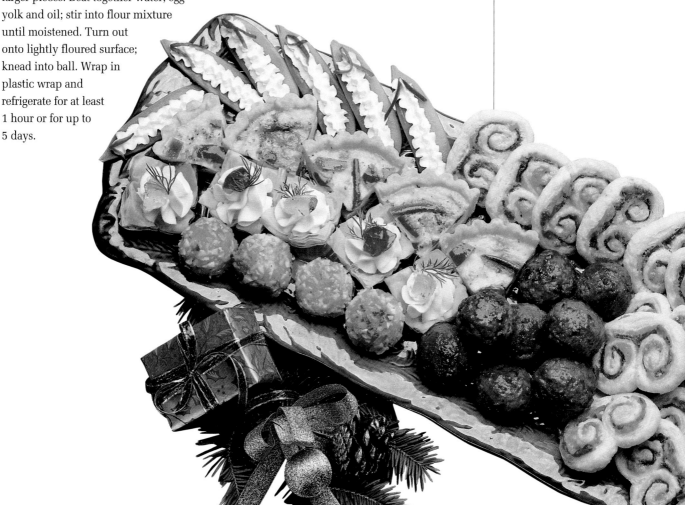

Mini Crab Quiches

Make-ahead appetizers, like these tartlets filled with a creamy filling that stays moist, are the key to stress-free entertaining (photo, p. 45).

Per piece: about
- 113 calories
- 3 g protein
- 7 g fat
- 8 g carbohydrate

	Perfect Pastry (recipe, p. 55)	
	FILLING	
1/2 cup	milk	125 mL
1/2 cup	herbed cream cheese	125 mL
2	eggs, beaten	2
1/4 tsp	each salt and hot pepper sauce	1 mL
Pinch	pepper	Pinch
1	pkg (7 oz/200 g) frozen crabmeat, thawed and drained	1
	Sliced green onions	

● On lightly floured surface, roll out pastry to 1/8-inch (3 mm) thickness; cut out thirty-six 5-inch (12 cm) rounds. Fit into 2-1/4-inch (6 cm) tart cups. With fork, prick each shell in several places. Refrigerate for 30 minutes. Bake in center of 375°F (190°C) oven for 15 minutes.

● FILLING: In saucepan, heat milk over medium-high heat until bubbles form around edge. Add cheese, stirring until melted. Remove from heat. In bowl, whisk 2 tbsp (25 mL) milk mixture into eggs; gradually add remaining milk mixture, stirring constantly. Stir in salt, hot pepper sauce and pepper; mix in crab.

● Spoon filling into pastry cups; bake for 12 minutes or until puffed and just set. Run knife around edges; remove from pan. *(Quiches can be frozen in single layers between waxed paper in rigid airtight container for up to 2 weeks. Reheat, frozen, on baking sheet in 375°F/190°C oven for 15 minutes.)* Garnish with onions. Makes 36 pieces.

TIP: Chilling and pricking tart shells before baking helps keep pastry tender and prevents shrinking.

Brie and Pecan Tartlets

Brie offers a delicious new taste twist on cheese in tarts.

Per piece: about
- 98 calories
- 2 g protein
- 6 g fat
- 8 g carbohydrate

Half	Perfect Pastry (recipe, p. 55)	Half
1	pkg (4-1/2 oz/125 g) Brie cheese	1
3 tbsp	finely chopped pecans	50 mL
3 tbsp	packed brown sugar	50 mL
2 tbsp	whisky or apple juice	25 mL

● On lightly floured surface, roll out pastry to 1/8-inch (3 mm) thickness; cut out twenty-four 3-inch (8 cm) rounds. Fit into 2-1/4-inch (6 cm) tart cups. With fork, prick each shell in several places. Refrigerate for 30 minutes.

● Bake in center of 375°F (190°C) oven for about 20 minutes or until golden and just cooked. Let cool on racks. *(Tart shells can be frozen in single layers and stored in rigid airtight containers for up to 2 weeks.)*

● Divide Brie into 24 wedges; place in baked tart shells. In saucepan, heat pecans, sugar and whisky over medium heat, stirring, until bubbly. Reduce heat and simmer for 1 minute or until thickened.

● Working quickly, spoon pecan mixture over Brie. *(Tarts can be prepared to this point, covered and refrigerated for up to 1 day; let stand at room temperature for 30 minutes before baking.)* Bake in center of 375°F (190°C) oven for 10 minutes or until hot and bubbly. Makes 24 pieces.

Hazelnut and Blue Cheese Tartlets

1/4 cup	toasted hazelnuts	50 mL
1 cup	all-purpose flour	250 mL
1/4 tsp	salt	1 mL
1/4 cup	cold butter, cubed	50 mL
1	egg yolk	1
1 tbsp	ice water	15 mL
	FILLING	
4 oz	cream cheese	125 g
1 oz	Roquefort cheese	30 g
1	egg	1
1 tbsp	milk	15 mL
1/4 tsp	pepper	1 mL
1/2 cup	chopped cooked spinach	125 mL
2 tbsp	chopped toasted hazelnuts	25 mL

● In food processor fitted with metal blade, chop hazelnuts with 1 tbsp (15 mL) of the flour just until fine. Add remaining flour and salt; using on/off motion, cut in butter until mixture resembles coarse crumbs.

● Whisk egg yolk with water; sprinkle over flour mixture. Using on/off motion, blend just until dough starts to form ball. Using floured hands, press dough together.

● Using small pieces of dough, press evenly into bottoms and up sides of 28 mini tart shells. Prick bottoms with fork; bake in center of 425°F (220°C) oven for 7 minutes. Let cool in pan on rack.

● FILLING: In food processor, combine cream cheese, Roquefort cheese, egg, milk and pepper; fold in spinach and hazelnuts. Spoon heaping 2 tsp (10 mL) filling into each shell. Bake in center of 325°F (160°C) oven for 10 minutes or until centers are firm. Makes 28 pieces.

Hazelnuts are in the pastry, and cheese is in the filling. Match these mini mouthfuls with port.

Per piece: about
- 68 calories
- 5 g fat
- 2 g protein
- 4 g carbohydrate

TIP: To toast hazelnuts, spread on baking sheet and bake in 350°F (180°C) oven for about 10 minutes or until fragrant. Transfer to tea towel and rub off as much of the skins as possible.

PERFECT PASTRY

Here's the basic beginner pastry that we teach in the Canadian Living Cooking School.

3 cups	all-purpose flour	750 mL
1 tsp	salt	5 mL
1/2 cup	cold butter, cubed	125 mL
1/2 cup	cold lard or shortening, cubed	125 mL
1	egg	1
2 tsp	white vinegar	10 mL
	Ice water	

● In bowl, combine flour and salt; with pastry blender or two knives, cut in butter and lard until crumbly. In measure, beat together egg and vinegar; add enough ice water to make 2/3 cup (150 mL). Drizzle all over flour mixture, tossing with fork until dough is evenly moistened and ragged.

● Press firmly into 2 rounds; wrap each in plastic wrap and refrigerate for at least 1 hour or until chilled. Let stand at room temperature for 10 minutes to soften slightly before rolling. *(Pastry can be refrigerated for up to 5 days.)* Makes enough for 1 double-crust or 2 single-crust pies or 48 small tarts.

Mushroom Crescents ▶

Exotic and button mushrooms accented with herbs are deliciously enrobed in an easy-to-handle cream cheese dough. These crescents don't stick around to get stale!

Per piece: about
- 45 calories
- 3 g fat
- 1 g protein
- 3 g carbohydrate

2 tbsp	butter	25 mL
1	small onion, chopped	1
3	cloves garlic, minced	3
3/4 tsp	each dried thyme and sage	4 mL
1/2 tsp	pepper	2 mL
1/4 tsp	salt	1 mL
1-1/2 cups	finely chopped portobello mushrooms (about 3 oz/90 g)	375 mL
1-1/2 cups	finely chopped button mushrooms (about 4 oz/125 g)	375 mL
1/3 cup	white wine or water	75 mL
	PASTRY	
1/2 cup	cream cheese, softened	125 mL
1/3 cup	butter, softened	75 mL
1 cup	all-purpose flour	250 mL
1	egg, beaten	1

● In large saucepan, melt butter over medium heat; cook onion, garlic, thyme, sage, pepper and salt, stirring occasionally, for 3 minutes or until onion is softened.

● Increase heat to medium-high. Add portobello and button mushrooms; cook, stirring occasionally, for 10 minutes or until browned. Stir in wine, scraping up brown bits from bottom of pan. Cook for about 5 minutes or until liquid is evaporated. Let cool to room temperature. *(Filling can be refrigerated in airtight container for up to 24 hours.)*

● PASTRY: In large bowl, beat cream cheese with butter until fluffy. Stir in flour until dough begins to form; knead in bowl until smooth. Divide in half and flatten into discs; wrap each in plastic wrap and refrigerate for at least 30 minutes or until firm. *(Pastry can be refrigerated for up to 2 days.)*

● On lightly floured surface, roll out each disc into 10-inch (25 cm) circle. With 2-1/2-inch (6 cm) round cookie cutter, cut out circles, rerolling scraps once. Working with 6 circles at a time, brush edges lightly with some of the egg. Place 1 tsp (5 mL) filling in center of each; fold dough over filling, pinching edges to seal. Place on ungreased baking sheet. Brush tops with remaining egg. *(Crescents can be frozen in single layers between waxed paper in rigid airtight container for up to 3 weeks; do not thaw.)*

● Bake in center of 400°F (200°C) oven for 12 to 15 minutes or until lightly golden. Serve warm or at room temperature. Makes about 40 pieces.

FLAKY PHYLLO CUPS

These cups are easy to make and freeze well, so consider making extra to use with other fillings such as the one in Smoked Salmon Éclairs (p. 61).

● Place one of six sheets of phyllo pastry on work surface, keeping remainder covered with damp towel to prevent drying out. Brush sheet lightly with melted butter (you will need approx 1/4 cup/50 mL melted butter in total).

● Top with 2 more sheets, brushing each lightly with butter. Cut lengthwise into 4 strips and crosswise into 6 strips to make 24 squares. Press each into lightly greased mini muffin or tart cups. Repeat with remaining phyllo to make 48 cups.

● Bake in center of 400°F (200°C) oven for about 5 minutes or until golden. Let cool in pan on rack. *(Phyllo cups can be frozen in single layers and stored in rigid airtight containers for up to 1 month; recrisp in 350°F/180°C oven for 3 minutes.)* Makes 48 phyllo cups.

Per phyllo cup: about • 17 calories • trace protein • 1 g fat • 2 g carbohydrate

(Clockwise from top) Beggar's Purse (p. 69), Thai Crab Salad Phyllo Cup, Mushroom Crescent (p. 56), Coconut Curried Chicken Phyllo Roll (p. 69)

Thai Crab Salad Phyllo Cups ▲

48	Flaky Phyllo Cups (recipe, p. 56)	48	2/3 cup	each finely chopped English cucumber and sweet red pepper	150 mL
2 tbsp	finely chopped peanuts	25 mL	3 tbsp	each finely chopped green onion and fresh basil or mint	50 mL
	FILLING				
3 tbsp	vegetable oil	50 mL			
3 tbsp	lime or lemon juice	50 mL			
2 tbsp	granulated sugar	25 mL			
4 tsp	fish sauce or soy sauce	20 mL			
1-1/2 tsp	peanut butter	7 mL			
1	clove garlic, minced	1			
Dash	hot pepper sauce	Dash			
8 oz	crabmeat (fresh or thawed)	250 g			

● FILLING: In large bowl, whisk together oil, lime juice, sugar, fish sauce, peanut butter, garlic and hot pepper sauce until sugar is dissolved. Gently squeeze any excess liquid from crab. Add crab to bowl along with cucumber, red pepper, onion and basil; toss to combine.

● Spoon filling into phyllo cups. Sprinkle with peanuts. Makes 48 pieces.

The fresh taste and cool colors of this salad filling lend an exotic glamor to an appetizer selection. To keep the phyllo cups from becoming soggy, spoon in the filling just before serving.

Per piece: about
- 38 calories
- 2 g fat
- 2 g protein
- 3 g carbohydrate

TIP: If desired, substitute salad shrimp for the crabmeat.

Roast Beef and Horseradish Phyllo Cups

A bit like mini sandwiches with a creamy but tangy filling, these intriguing little tartlets taste best made with very thinly sliced rare roast beef.

Per piece: about
- 40 calories
- 2 g protein
- 3 g fat
- 2 g carbohydrate

2/3 cup	spreadable cream cheese	150 mL
2 tbsp	horseradish	25 mL
1-1/2 tsp	grainy or Dijon mustard	7 mL
1/2 tsp	Worcestershire sauce	2 mL
48	thin slices English cucumber (about 4 inches/10 cm long)	48
8 oz	shaved rare roast beef	250 g
48	Flaky Phyllo Cups (recipe, page 56)	48

● In small bowl, blend together cream cheese, horseradish, mustard and Worcestershire sauce; set aside.

● Cut cucumber slices in half. Trim any fat from beef; cut into forty-eight 2- x 1-1/2-inch (5 x 4 cm) pieces. Spoon rounded 1/2 tsp (2 mL) cheese mixture into each phyllo cup. Arrange 2 cucumber pieces on either side of each cup. Fold each piece of beef in half lengthwise; crumple loosely and fit into cup between cucumber. Makes 48 pieces.

Savory Phyllo Cups

Crisp little cups are filled with cream cheese and accented with the pleasurable warmth of pepper jelly (photo, p. 53).

Per piece: about
- 47 calories
- 1 g protein
- 3 g fat
- 4 g carbohydrate

3/4 cup	cream cheese	175 mL
2 tbsp	butter, softened	25 mL
48	Flaky Phyllo Cups (recipe, p. 56)	48
1/2 cup	jalapeño or homemade hot pepper jelly	125 mL
	Dill sprigs	

● In food processor or bowl, blend cream cheese with butter until smooth; pipe or spoon into phyllo cups. Top each with about 1/4 tsp (1 mL) jalapeño jelly; garnish with dill. *(Phyllo cups can be covered and refrigerated for up to 24 hours; let stand at room temperature for 45 minutes before serving.)* Makes about 50 pieces.

VARIATION

● SMOKED SALMON PHYLLO CUPS: Add about 2 oz (60 g) smoked salmon to cream cheese and butter; process until smooth. Omit jalapeño jelly.

Guacamole Tartlets

Amid all the baked fillings, a fresh and colorful avocado filling is a delight to the senses.

Per piece with tomatoes: about
- 114 calories
- 1 g protein
- 8 g fat
- 10 g carbohydrate

Per piece with cheese: about
- 129 calories
- 2 g protein
- 9 g fat
- 10 g carbohydrate

Half	small tomato, seeded and diced	Half
1	clove garlic, minced	1
1 tbsp	lime juice	15 mL
Pinch	each salt and pepper	Pinch
Dash	hot pepper sauce	Dash
1	ripe avocado	1
3	cherry tomatoes	3
2 oz	Brie cheese	60 g
24	baked tart shells	24
	Parsley sprigs	

● In bowl, combine tomato, garlic, lime juice, salt, pepper and hot pepper sauce. Peel, pit and dice avocado; add to bowl and mash until spreadable. *(Guacamole can be covered and refrigerated for up to 8 hours.)*

● Just before serving, quarter cherry tomatoes; cut Brie into 12 triangles. Fill tart shells with guacamole. Garnish half with cherry tomatoes and half with cheese and parsley. Makes 24 pieces.

Rosemary Parmesan Shortbread Bites

1/2 cup	butter, softened	125 mL
2 tsp	granulated sugar	10 mL
1 cup	all-purpose flour	250 mL
1/4 cup	freshly grated Parmesan cheese	50 mL
2 tsp	crushed dried rosemary (or 2 tbsp/25 mL chopped fresh)	10 mL
1/2 tsp	paprika	2 mL

● In bowl, beat butter with sugar until light and fluffy. Combine flour, Parmesan cheese, rosemary and paprika; stir into flour mixture, mixing with hands to form dough that holds together.

● Divide dough into thirds. On lightly floured surface, roll each piece into 12-inch (30 cm) rope; cut into 1/2-inch (1 cm) pieces.

● Place on baking sheet; bake in center of 350°F (180°C) oven for 14 to 16 minutes or until golden. Let cool on pan on rack. *(Bites can be stored in rigid airtight container for up to 5 days or frozen for up to 2 weeks. To serve, warm in 350°F/180°C oven for 3 to 5 minutes.)* Makes about 48 pieces.

M*ake plenty of these savory nuggets to serve with an aperitif. They're a delicious change from the usual spiced or salty nuts.*

Per piece: about
● 30 calories   ● 1 g protein
● 2 g fat   ● 2 g carbohydrate

Jalapeño Stars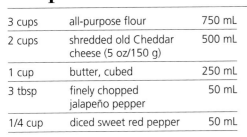

3 cups	all-purpose flour	750 mL
2 cups	shredded old Cheddar cheese (5 oz/150 g)	500 mL
1 cup	butter, cubed	250 mL
3 tbsp	finely chopped jalapeño pepper	50 mL
1/4 cup	diced sweet red pepper	50 mL

● In food processor or bowl, combine flour and cheese. Add butter, jalapeño pepper and red pepper; pulse or cut in with pastry blender until ball forms. Between sheets of waxed paper, roll out dough to 1/4-inch (5 mm) thickness.

● Using star-shaped cookie cutters of various sizes, cut out about 45 stars; transfer to ungreased baking sheets. Bake in center of 350°F (180°C) oven for 15 to 20 minutes or until golden brown.

● Transfer to racks and let cool slightly. Serve warm or at room temperature. *(Stars can be refrigerated in rigid airtight containers for up to 5 days or frozen for up to 3 weeks; reheat for 5 to 10 minutes to serve.)* Makes about 45 pieces.

U*se star-shape or other cookie cutters to update cheese shortbread coins.*

Per piece: about
● 80 calories   ● 2 g protein
● 5 g fat   ● 7 g carbohydrate

Savory Cheddar Thumbprint Cookies (left) and Smoked Salmon Éclairs

Savory Cheddar Thumbprint Cookies ▲

Bejewelled with pepper jelly and studded with chopped nuts, these cookies look sweet but are distinctly savory. The food processor provides a timesaving shortcut.

Per piece: about
- 101 calories
- 3 g protein
- 7 g fat
- 8 g carbohydrate

1-1/2 cups	shredded white old Cheddar cheese	375 mL
1/2 cup	freshly grated Parmesan cheese	125 mL
1/2 cup	butter, softened	125 mL
1	egg yolk	1
1/4 tsp	pepper	1 mL
1 cup	all-purpose flour	250 mL
1 cup	finely chopped pecans or unblanched almonds	250 mL
3/4 cup	hot pepper jelly	175 mL

● In food processor, pulse together Cheddar and Parmesan cheeses and butter until smooth. Add egg yolk and pepper; pulse until blended. Add flour; pulse just until soft dough forms.

● Place pecans on plate. Place 1 cup (250 mL) water in bowl. With hands, roll scant tablespoonfuls (15 mL) of dough into 1-inch (2.5 cm) balls. Dip in water; roll in nuts to coat. Place on ungreased baking sheet. With thumb, make indentation in center of each. Refrigerate for 15 minutes.

● Bake in center of 350°F (180°C) oven for about 15 minutes or until firm outside and lightly golden. Let cool on baking sheet on rack. *(Cookies can be prepared to this point and frozen in layers separated by waxed paper in rigid airtight container for up to 2 weeks; bake in 350°F/180°C oven for about 3 minutes to recrisp.)* Fill indentations with hot pepper jelly. Makes about 36 pieces.

Smoked Salmon Éclairs ◀

1/2 cup	water	125 mL
1/4 cup	butter	50 mL
Pinch	salt	Pinch
2/3 cup	all-purpose flour	150 mL
2	eggs	2
	GLAZE	
1	egg, lightly beaten	1
	FILLING	
3/4 cup	cream cheese, softened	175 mL
4 oz	smoked salmon, chopped	125 g
4 tsp	chopped fresh dill	20 mL
2 tsp	lemon juice	10 mL
	GARNISH	
	Fresh dill sprigs	

● In saucepan, bring water, butter and salt to boil over high heat just until butter is melted; remove from heat. Add flour all at once; stir vigorously with wooden spoon until dough comes away from side of pan and forms ball.

● Return to medium heat; cook, stirring, for 2 minutes or until film begins to form on bottom of pan. Transfer to bowl; stir for 30 seconds to cool slightly.

● Make well in center. Using electric mixer, beat in eggs, one at a time, beating until pastry is shiny and holds its shape when beaters are lifted.

● Using pastry bag fitted with 1/4-inch (5 mm) plain tip, pipe pastry into 2- x 1/2-inch (5 x 1 cm) strips about 1 inch (2.5 cm) apart onto two parchment paper-lined or greased and floured baking sheets.

● GLAZE: Brush egg over éclairs. Bake in center of 425°F (220°C) oven for 15 minutes. Reduce heat to 375°F (190°C); bake for 5 minutes. Turn off oven. With tip of small knife, pierce each at side; let dry in oven for 5 minutes. Transfer to rack; let cool. *(Unfilled éclairs can be frozen in layers separated by waxed paper in rigid airtight container for up to 1 month.)*

● FILLING: In bowl, mix together cream cheese, salmon, dill and lemon juice. With serrated knife, slice off top half of each éclair. Spoon rounded teaspoonful (5 mL) into each bottom; replace tops. Garnish with dill. Makes 36 pieces.

VARIATION
● SMOKED SALMON PHYLLO CUPS: Prepare filling as directed; spoon into 36 Flaky Phyllo Cups (recipe, p. 56).

Choux pastry freezes like a dream, and with unfilled mini éclairs in the freezer, it's extra-easy and fast to whip up impressive appetizers like these. The filling is smoked salmon blended into cream cheese, but a prepared herb cream cheese could also be used in a hurried moment.

Per piece: about
● 47 calories ● 2 g protein
● 4 g fat ● 2 g carbohydrate

Wraps and Vegetable Bites

Here's a platterful of pleasers — from tasty tortilla wraps and phyllo packets to extra-easy mini stuffed tomatoes.

Classy Crêpe Cones ▶

No festive food is more versatile, affordable and delectable than lacy crêpes. Serve them as holiday appetizers, shaped into cones and deliciously stuffed with salmon and cream cheese.

Per piece: about
- 52 calories
- 4 g fat
- 2 g protein
- 3 g carbohydrate

TIP: To serve cones warm, arrange filled crêpes, seam side down, in two 13- x 9-inch (3 L) baking dishes; cover and bake in 350°F (180°C) oven for 5 to 10 minutes or until heated through.

1 cup	all-purpose flour	250 mL
1/4 tsp	salt	1 mL
3	eggs	3
1-1/4 cups	milk	300 mL
3 tbsp	(approx) butter, melted	50 mL
	FILLING	
8 oz	cream cheese, softened	250 g
1/2 cup	sour cream	125 mL
1/4 cup	chopped fresh dill	50 mL
1	clove garlic, minced	1
1	green onion, finely chopped	1
1/2 tsp	grated lemon rind	2 mL
	Salt and pepper	
1 cup	watercress leaves (or 2 cups/500 mL coarsely chopped spinach)	250 mL
8 oz	thinly sliced smoked salmon, cut in strips	250 g
48	watercress or parsley sprigs	48

● In bowl, combine flour and salt; make well in center. Whisk together eggs, milk and 2 tbsp (25 mL) of the butter; gradually pour into well, whisking to draw in flour until smooth. Cover and refrigerate for 1 hour. Strain to give smooth, whipping-cream consistency.

● Heat 8-inch (20 cm) crêpe pan over medium heat until drop of water sprinkled on pan spatters briskly. Brush with some of the remaining butter. Stir batter to reblend; pour 2 tbsp (25 mL) into center of pan. Quickly tilt and rotate pan to form thin crêpe. Cook for 40 seconds or until bottom is golden and top no longer shiny. Loosen and turn crêpe over; cook for 30 seconds or until golden. Transfer to plate.

● Repeat with remaining batter, brushing pan with butter as necessary and stacking crêpes on plate. *(Crêpes can be layered between waxed paper, wrapped in plastic wrap and refrigerated for up to 3 days or frozen in rigid airtight container for up to 2 months.)*

● FILLING: In bowl, combine cream cheese, sour cream, dill, garlic, onion, lemon rind, and salt and pepper to taste. Working in batches, spread paler side of each crêpe with 1 tbsp (15 mL) filling, leaving 1/2-inch (1 cm) border. Cut in half; top with watercress leaves and salmon.

● Forming point at center of straight edge of crêpe, roll into cone. *(Cones can be covered and refrigerated for up to 4 hours; let stand at room temperature for 30 minutes before serving.)* Garnish each cone with watercress sprig. Makes 48 pieces.

Roast Beef and Olive Rolls

Toronto food writer Bonnie Stern rolls up thinly sliced roast beef in a tortilla and transforms a popular sandwich into attractive party fare. Black olive paste is available in Italian or specialty food stores.

Per piece: about
- 56 calories
- 3 g protein
- 3 g fat
- 4 g carbohydrate

3/4 cup	black olive paste or finely chopped pitted black olives	175 mL
1/2 cup	mayonnaise	125 mL
8	10-inch (25 cm) flour tortillas	8
1 lb	thinly sliced rare roast beef	500 g
4 cups	shredded romaine lettuce	1 L

● In bowl, combine olive paste with mayonnaise; spread over tortillas. Cover with slices of meat, leaving 1-inch (2.5 cm) border at one end. Top with lettuce.

● Starting at end with meat, roll up tightly, sealing border with mayonnaise mixture. Wrap tightly and refrigerate for up to 4 hours.

● Cut each roll into 8 slices; arrange, cut sides up, on platter. Makes 60 pieces.

Tortilla Roll-Ups

Asparagus and beef team up with zippy cream cheese in a tasty tortilla wrap (photo, p. 20).

Per piece: about
- 125 calories
- 7 g protein
- 4 g fat
- 15 g carbohydrate

1/3 cup	light cream cheese, softened	75 mL
1 tbsp	horseradish	15 mL
6	flour tortillas 8-inch (20 cm)	6
6	halves roasted red peppers	6
6	thin slices cooked roast beef	6
6	asparagus spears, blanched	6

● In small bowl, whisk cream cheese with horseradish; spread evenly over tortillas. Top each with red pepper half; lay beef slice on top. Place asparagus on 1 side; starting from asparagus side, roll up, jelly roll-style. Secure with toothpick. *(Roll-Ups can be covered and refrigerated for up to 1 hour.)* Cut in half to serve. Makes 12 appetizers.

QUICK TORTILLA TRICKS
Need an appetizer in a hurry? Let versatile tortillas come to the rescue.

Make Quesadillas
Start with four tortillas, sprinkle half with a cheese that melts, then build.

● Try Brie with toasted pecans and chutney, Fontina with grilled or roasted vegetables, Gouda with smoky ham and thinly sliced dills or with drained coleslaw, Havarti with cranberry sauce, Monterey Jack with drained rinsed red kidney beans or black beans and salsa, Cheddar with chopped red onion and sweet red pepper, mozzarella or provolone with chopped sweet green pepper and pepperoni.

● Don't fill too full. Fold over and cook in nonstick skillet or on grill, turning once, until crisp on the outside and melty inside.

Roll Tortillas
Spread with something that will hold the spiral.

● Try light cream cheese, herbed if you like, plus smoked salmon, chopped fresh dill or capers plus sprouts. Or top with chopped smoked oysters, sardines or cooked asparagus, or chopped roasted peppers and olives. Another sticking spread is a light mayonnaise mixed with mustard, then topped with shaved ham or roast beef.

● Roll firmly, wrap in plastic wrap and refrigerate if time allows. Cut on diagonal into nibble-size slices.

● If you like, make a line of fillings — including crisp foods such as sprouts or lettuce — about one-third up a tortilla spread with cream cheese. Top with cooked shrimp, crab or lobster, smoked oysters or mussels, and roll for a centered filling.

Pesto Spirals

2 tbsp	pesto	25 mL
2	10-inch (25 cm) flour tortillas	2
4 oz	cream goat cheese (chèvre) or herb cream cheese	125 g
1	jar (11 oz/313 mL) roasted red peppers, drained	1

● Spread pesto along edge of one side of each tortilla to resemble sliver of moon. Spread goat cheese over remaining tortilla. Starting beside pesto, cover center of each with red peppers, leaving 2-inch (5 cm) border of cheese uncovered at edge opposite pesto. Starting at pesto side, roll up. Wrap each in plastic wrap; refrigerate for 1 hour or for up to 24 hours. Cut each roll diagonally into 12 slices. Makes 24 pieces.

D*iagonal slices of this tortilla reveal bright red pepper and vivid green pesto.*

Per piece: about
- 35 calories
- 1 g protein
- 2 g fat
- 3 g carbohydrate

Wasabi Bites

2 tbsp	light mayonnaise	25 mL
1/2 tsp	wasabi paste or horseradish	2 mL
6	thin slices cooked roast beef or steak	6
1 cup	watercress leaves or torn arugula	250 mL
Half	carrot, julienned	Half

● In small bowl, stir mayonnaise with wasabi; spread evenly over beef. Sprinkle watercress over top. Arrange 3 or 4 pieces of carrot on 1 side of beef; starting from carrot side, roll up, jelly roll-style. Secure with toothpick. *(Rolls can be covered and refrigerated for up to 2 hours.)* Makes 6 appetizers.

W*asabi, a Japanese version of horseradish, is available in specialty food stores.*

Per appetizer: about
- 80 calories
- 9 g protein
- 4 g fat
- 1 g carbohydrate

Rice-Paper Spring Rolls

2 oz	rice noodles	60 g
12	large cooked shrimp	12
12	small rice-paper wrappers	12
12	small leaves leaf lettuce	12
3/4 cup	bean sprouts, chopped	175 mL
1/2 cup	julienned cooked lean pork	125 mL
2 tbsp	chopped roasted peanuts	25 mL
1/4 cup	chopped fresh coriander	50 mL
	SAUCE	
1/2 cup	hoisin sauce	125 mL
1/4 cup	water	50 mL
1 tbsp	granulated sugar	15 mL
1/2 tsp	cornstarch	2 mL

● SAUCE: In saucepan, cook hoisin sauce, water, sugar and cornstarch over medium heat, stirring, until thickened. Set aside.

● In saucepan of lightly salted boiling water, cook noodles, separating with fork, for 2 to 3 minutes or until opaque. Drain and cool under cold water. Slice each shrimp in half lengthwise.

● Working with 1 wrapper at a time, dip into hand-hot water for 20 seconds or until just softened. Lay flat on dampened towel. Place piece of lettuce on wrapper about 1 inch (2.5 cm) from edge. Top with one-twelfth each of the bean sprouts and noodles. Place 2 shrimp halves beside noodles; top with one-twelfth of the pork. Drizzle with 1/2 tsp (2 mL) sauce. Sprinkle with about 1/2 tsp (2 mL) of the peanuts and 3/4 tsp (4 mL) of the coriander. Fold up bottom edge of wrapper, then sides; roll up. Repeat with remaining ingredients. Serve with remaining sauce. Makes 12 rolls.

A *fresh salad is rolled for easy eating in softened rice-paper wrappers. Look for the wrappers and rice noodles in Asian food stores.*

Per roll: about
- 92 calories
- 5 g protein
- 2 g fat
- 14 g carbohydrate

Crispy Spring Rolls ◄

8	dried Chinese black mushrooms	8
12 oz	boneless pork loin	375 g
12 oz	raw shrimp	375 g
2 tbsp	sesame oil	25 mL
1 tbsp	vegetable oil	15 mL
1	clove garlic, minced	1
1 tsp	minced gingerroot	5 mL
2 cups	shredded Chinese (napa) cabbage	500 mL
1 cup	bean sprouts	250 mL
1/2 cup	water chestnuts, slivered	125 mL
4	green onions, sliced	4
2 tbsp	oyster sauce	25 mL
1 tbsp	soy sauce	15 mL
1/2 tsp	salt	2 mL
2 tsp	cornstarch	10 mL
1	pkg 6-inch (15 cm) frozen spring roll wrappers	1
2	egg whites	2
	Vegetable oil for deep-frying	

DIPPING SAUCE		
1/3 cup	plum sauce	75 mL
1 tbsp	lemon juice	15 mL
1/2 tsp	Asian chili sauce or paste	2 mL
1	clove garlic, minced	1

● In small bowl, soak mushrooms in warm water for 20 minutes; drain. Cut off and discard tough stems; chop caps finely and set aside. Slice pork thinly across the grain; chop finely. Peel and devein shrimp; chop coarsely.

● In wok or skillet, heat sesame and vegetable oils over high heat; stir-fry pork, shrimp, garlic and ginger for 2 minutes or until pork is no longer pink. Add mushrooms, cabbage, bean sprouts, water chestnuts, onions, oyster and soy sauces and salt; stir-fry for 3 minutes.

● Push mixture to side of wok. Blend cornstarch with 2 tsp (10 mL) water; pour into liquid in wok and cook, stirring, for 1 minute or until thickened. Stir vegetable mixture back into liquid. Transfer to large bowl; refrigerate for 1 hour or until cooled completely.

● Working with 1 spring roll wrapper at a time and keeping remainder covered with damp tea towel, lay wrapper on work surface with one corner toward you. Place 3 tbsp (50 mL) filling about 2 inches (5 cm) from corner. Fold corner over filling. Brush remaining edges with egg white. Fold in both sides and roll up firmly into cylinder.

● In wok, Dutch oven or deep-fryer, heat oil over high heat until deep-frying thermometer registers 375°F (190°C) or 1-inch (2.5 cm) cube of white bread turns golden in 40 seconds.

● Deep-fry rolls, in batches of 4, for 4 to 5 minutes or until golden, turning once. Remove with tongs or slotted spoon; drain well on paper towels. *(Spring rolls can be cooled and frozen in rigid airtight container for up to 1 month; to reheat, bake, frozen, on baking sheet in 375°F/190°C oven for 20 minutes or until hot.)*

● DIPPING SAUCE: Combine plum sauce, lemon juice, chili sauce and garlic. Serve with spring rolls. Makes 24 rolls.

These crunchy shrimp spring rolls were once considered too fussy for home cooks. Today, with the advent of frozen wrappers and the availability of Asian ingredients in supermarkets, they're a snap to make.

Per roll: about
• 91 calories
• 4 g fat
• 7 g protein
• 8 g carbohydrate

TIP: Look for frozen spring roll wrappers, called lumpia skins or Shanghai wrappers, in Asian stores. If unavailable, you can use the thicker egg roll wrappers, but the rolls won't be as crispy.

PHYLLO WRAP PARTY

Gather friends together for a party in the kitchen. Make these favorite buffet appetizers filled with a trio of fabulous flavors — seasonal tourtière, spicy southwest-accented bean and salsa, and savory ham and cheese. The appetizers freeze beautifully — ready to go into the oven when needed for a holiday party, wedding, shower or graduation.

PHYLLO APPETIZERS

16	sheets phyllo pastry	16
1/2 cup	butter, melted	125 mL
	Tourtière Filling, Bean and Salsa Filling or Ham and Swiss Filling (recipes follow)	

● Place 1 sheet of the phyllo on work surface, keeping remainder covered with damp towel to prevent drying out. Cut sheet lengthwise into five 2-1/2-inch (6 cm) wide strips; brush lightly with butter.

● Spoon heaping teaspoonful (5 mL) filling about 1/2 inch (1 cm) from end of each strip. Fold one corner of phyllo over filling so bottom edge meets side edge to form triangle; fold up triangle. Continue folding triangle sideways and upward until at end of strip; fold end flap over to adhere. Repeat with remaining phyllo and filling.

● Brush triangles on both sides with butter. Place on baking sheet; let cool until butter is hardened. *(Triangles can be frozen and stored in layers between waxed paper in rigid airtight containers for up to 1 week; do not thaw.)* Bake in center of 375°F (190°C) oven for 15 to 18 minutes for fresh, 20 minutes for frozen, or until golden and piping hot. Makes about 80 pieces.

Per piece with Bean and Salsa Filling: about • 39 calories • 1 g protein • 1 g fat • 6 g carbohydrate

Per piece with Ham and Swiss Filling: about • 46 calories • 2 g protein • 2 g fat • 4 g carbohydrate

Per piece with Tourtière Filling: about • 53 calories • 3 g protein • 3 g fat • 4 g carbohydrate

BEAN AND SALSA FILLING

2	cans (19 oz/540 mL each) black beans	2
1-1/2 cups	medium salsa	375 mL
1-1/2	sweet red peppers, chopped	1-1/2
1/2 cup	corn kernels	125 mL
1/4 cup	chopped fresh coriander or parsley	50 mL

● Drain and rinse beans; place in large bowl and mash about half with fork or potato masher. Stir in salsa, red peppers and corn. *(Filling can be refrigerated in airtight container for up to 24 hours.)* Stir in coriander. Makes about 5 cups (1.25 L), enough for about 80 pieces.

HAM AND SWISS FILLING

3 cups	shredded Black Forest ham (1 lb/500 g)	750 mL
3 cups	shredded Swiss cheese (8 oz/250 g)	750 mL
2	large tart apples, peeled and grated	2
3 tbsp	Dijon mustard	50 mL
1-1/2 tsp	pepper	7 mL

● In large bowl, toss together ham, cheese and apples. Combine mustard, 2 tbsp (25 mL) water and pepper; pour over ham mixture and toss until thoroughly moistened. *(Filling can be refrigerated in airtight container for up to 24 hours.)* Makes about 5 cups (1.25 L), enough for about 80 pieces.

TOURTIÈRE FILLING

1 tbsp	vegetable oil	15 mL
1-3/4 lb	ground pork, chicken or turkey	875 g
1-1/3 cups	chicken stock	325 mL
2	onions, chopped	2
2	cloves garlic, minced	2
1/2 tsp	each pepper, dried thyme and cinnamon	2 mL
1/4 tsp	each salt and dried savory	1 mL
3/4 cup	grated carrot	175 mL
1 cup	fresh bread crumbs	250 mL
1/4 cup	chopped fresh parsley	50 mL

● In large skillet, heat oil over medium-high heat; cook pork, breaking up with wooden spoon, for 8 to 10 minutes or until no longer pink.

● Stir in stock, onions, garlic, pepper, thyme, cinnamon, salt and savory; reduce heat, cover and simmer for 20 minutes or until onions are softened. Stir in carrot; simmer, covered, for 5 minutes or until tender. Remove from heat. Stir in bread crumbs and parsley. *(Filling can be refrigerated in airtight container for up to 24 hours.)* Makes about 5 cups (1.25 L), enough for about 80 pieces.

Coconut Curried Chicken Phyllo Rolls ▼

1 lb	boneless skinless chicken breasts	500 g
1/2 tsp	cornstarch	2 mL
3/4 cup	light coconut milk	175 mL
1 tsp	vegetable oil	5 mL
4 tsp	mild curry paste or powder	20 mL
4 tsp	strained mango chutney	20 mL
1 tbsp	lemon or lime juice	15 mL
1/3 cup	dried currants (optional)	75 mL
2 tbsp	chopped fresh coriander	25 mL
2 tbsp	toasted ground almonds	25 mL
11	sheets phyllo pastry	11
1/3 cup	butter, melted	75 mL
55	fresh coriander leaves	55

● Pour water into large skillet to depth of 2 inches (5 cm); bring to boil. Add chicken; reduce heat and simmer for about 10 minutes or just until no longer pink inside. Drain and let cool; cut into 1/4-inch (5 mm) dice. Set aside.

● Whisk cornstarch into coconut milk; set aside. In skillet, heat oil over medium heat; cook curry paste, stirring, for 1 minute. Stir in coconut milk and bring to boil, stirring. Stir in chutney and lemon juice just until chutney is dissolved.

● Remove from heat. Stir in chicken, dried currants (if using), chopped coriander and almonds; let cool. *(Filling can be refrigerated in airtight container for up to 12 hours.)*

● Place 1 sheet of the phyllo on work surface, keeping remainder covered with damp towel to prevent drying out. Cut sheet lengthwise into five 2-1/2-inch (6 cm) wide strips; brush lightly with butter. Spoon heaping teaspoonful (5 mL) filling about 1/2 inch (1 cm) from one end and sides of each strip. Place coriander leaf in same position at other end. Fold both long sides over center, covering filling and leaf. Fold end border over filling and roll up to other end. Brush lightly with butter.

● Place on baking sheet; let cool until butter is hardened. Repeat with remaining phyllo. *(Rolls can be frozen, then stored in layers separated by waxed paper in rigid airtight container for up to 1 week; do not thaw.)*

● Bake in center of 375°F (190°C) oven for 15 to 18 minutes for fresh, 20 minutes for frozen, or until golden and crispy. Serve warm or at room temperature. Makes about 55 pieces.

*S*picy with a tad of sweetness, these delicately pretty morsels have a creamy consistency that comes from the coconut milk.

Per piece: about
- 39 calories
- 2 g fat
- 2 g protein
- 3 g carbohydrate

TIP: You can use regular coconut milk instead of the light. If you can't find either, substitute whipping cream; dissolve cornstarch in 1 tsp (5 mL) water.

BEGGAR'S PURSES
Instead of shaping into triangles or rolls, you can bake up phyllo appetizers into attractive little pouches (photo, p. 57).
● Use 9 sheets of phyllo and 1/3 cup (75 mL) butter, melted. Stack 3 sheets, brushing butter on first and second sheet; cut into 12 squares. Place heaping teaspoonful (5 mL) filling in center of each; bring up corners, pinching above filling to secure, or tie with strip of chive or green onion.

Phyllo Triangles ◀

10	sheets phyllo pastry	10
1/2 cup	butter, melted	125 mL
	SPINACH-CHEESE FILLING	
1 tbsp	olive oil	15 mL
2 tbsp	minced onion	25 mL
2	cloves garlic, minced	2
1 cup	ricotta cheese	250 mL
3/4 cup	chopped drained cooked spinach (10 oz/284 g pkg fresh)	175 mL
1/3 cup	freshly grated Parmesan cheese	75 mL
1/2 tsp	grated lemon rind	2 mL
Pinch	each salt, pepper and nutmeg	Pinch

● SPINACH-CHEESE FILLING: In skillet, heat oil over medium-high heat; cook onion and garlic, stirring occasionally, for 2 minutes or until softened. In bowl, stir together onion mixture, ricotta cheese, spinach, Parmesan cheese, lemon rind, salt, pepper and nutmeg; set aside.

● Place 1 sheet of the phyllo on work surface, keeping remainder covered with damp towel to prevent drying out. Cut sheet lengthwise into five 2-1/2-inch (6 cm) wide strips; brush lightly with butter.

● Spoon heaping teaspoonful (5 mL) filling about 1/2 inch (1 cm) from end of each strip. Fold one corner of phyllo over filling so bottom edge meets side edge to form triangle. Fold up triangle. Continue folding triangle sideways and upward until at end of strip; fold end flap over to adhere. Repeat with remaining phyllo and filling. Place on baking sheets.

● Brush triangles lightly with butter. *(Triangles can be frozen, then layered between waxed paper and stored in rigid airtight containers for up to 1 month; do not thaw.)* Bake in center of 375°F (190°C) oven for 15 to 18 minutes or until golden. Serve hot. Makes 50 pieces.

VARIATION
● MUSHROOM-SAUSAGE-CHEESE FILLING: Increase olive oil to 2 tbsp (25 mL). Add 2-1/2 cups (625 mL) chopped mushrooms and 1/4 tsp (1 mL) hot pepper flakes to sautéed onion mixture; cook, stirring, for 3 to 5 minutes or until mushrooms are tender. Transfer to bowl. To skillet, add 8 oz (250 g) crumbled hot Italian sausage; cook, stirring, for 3 to 5 minutes or until golden. Add to bowl along with remaining ingredients, but omit spinach and nutmeg. Use 1-1/2 tsp (7 mL) filling per triangle.

Guests won't be able to resist helping themselves to "just one more" of this flaky, paper-thin appetizer.

Per piece: about
- 46 calories
- 1 g protein
- 3 g fat
- 3 g carbohydrate

TIPS
● A 1 lb (454 g) package of frozen phyllo pastry usually contains 20 sheets. To thaw, place the package in the refrigerator for about 24 hours. It's best to refreeze any remaining phyllo only once.
● If phyllo tears while working with it, mend it by patching torn sections together with melted butter.

Asparagus Strudel

Serving a hot crispy appetizer on lightly dressed salad greens is very trendy — and very delicious. The recipe doubles and triples easily for a larger get-together.

Per serving: about
- 270 calories
- 20 g fat
- 6 g protein
- 17 g carbohydrate

1-1/2 cups	julienned leeks	375 mL
1/4 cup	cream goat cheese (chèvre) or cream cheese, softened	50 mL
1 tbsp	grated orange rind	15 mL
1 tbsp	orange juice	15 mL
1 tsp	dried tarragon (or 1 tbsp/15 mL chopped fresh)	5 mL
1/2 tsp	pepper	2 mL
	Salt	
4	sheets phyllo pastry	4
1/3 cup	butter, melted	75 mL
12	cooked asparagus spears, cut in half (approx 8 oz/250 g)	12

● In saucepan of boiling salted water, cook leeks for 1 minute. Drain and cool under cold water; drain again and set aside. In small bowl, combine goat cheese, orange rind and juice, tarragon, pepper, and salt to taste; set aside.

● Place 1 sheet of the phyllo on work surface, keeping remainder covered with damp towel to prevent drying out; brush lightly with some of the butter. Center 2 tbsp (25 mL) of the leeks about 1 inch (2.5 cm) from short edge; top with 3 pieces of asparagus. Spread 1 tbsp (15 mL) cheese mixture over asparagus. Top with 3 more asparagus pieces, then 2 tbsp (25 mL) of the leeks.

● Fold long sides of phyllo over mixture; brush phyllo with butter and roll up into cylinder. Place, seam side down, on greased baking sheet; brush with butter. Repeat with remaining ingredients to make 3 more rolls. *(Strudels can be prepared to this point, covered and refrigerated for up to 24 hours.)*

● Bake in center of 450°F (230°C) oven for about 12 minutes or until golden brown. Cut each roll into thirds just before serving hot. Makes about 4 servings.

Creamy Cheese Pear Pouches

Here's another deliciously inspired way to pinch and fold phyllo attractively.

Per piece: about
- 73 calories
- 5 g fat
- 2 g protein
- 4 g carbohydrate

1 cup	cream goat cheese (chèvre) or herb-and-garlic cream cheese	250 mL
2/3 cup	finely chopped peeled pear	150 mL
1/4 cup	toasted chopped almonds or walnuts	50 mL
2 tbsp	chopped fresh parsley	25 mL
Pinch	pepper	Pinch
6	sheets phyllo pastry	6
1/4 cup	butter, melted	50 mL
2 tbsp	Dijon mustard	25 mL

● In bowl, combine cheese, pear, nuts, parsley and pepper. Place 1 sheet of the phyllo on work surface, keeping remainder covered with damp towel to prevent drying out; brush lightly with some of the butter.

Top with second sheet; brush with half of the mustard. Lay third sheet on top; brush with butter. Turn over and butter other side.

● Cut lengthwise into thirds; cut crosswise into quarters to make 12 squares. Spoon about 2 tsp (10 mL) filling onto center of each; bring up corners, gathering up sides and pinching tightly at top to form pouch. Repeat with remaining phyllo. Place on baking sheets. *(Pouches can be covered and refrigerated for up to 1 day or frozen and stored in rigid airtight containers for up to 1 month; do not thaw.)*

● Bake in center of 375°F (190°C) oven for 15 to 20 minutes or until golden. Makes 24 pieces.

New Potatoes with Smoked Salmon

24	tiny (unpeeled) red new potatoes (1-1/2 lb/750 g)	24
1/4 cup	cream cheese, softened	50 mL
1/4 cup	sour cream	50 mL
4 tsp	chopped fresh dill	20 mL
Pinch	each salt and pepper	Pinch
1-1/2 oz	thinly sliced smoked salmon, cut in strips	45 g
24	dill sprigs or capers	24

● In pot of boiling water, cook potatoes for 16 to 20 minutes or until tender; let cool. Scoop out small spoonful of pulp from center of each potato.

● In bowl, combine cream cheese, sour cream, dill, salt and pepper; spoon about 1 tsp (5 mL) into each potato. Place on plate; cover with plastic wrap and refrigerate for at least 1 hour or for up to 8 hours.

● To serve, top each potato with strip of salmon; garnish with dill sprig. Makes 24 pieces.

Tiny freshly dug new potatoes are tasty holders of sour cream and something smoky — here salmon, but trout, oysters and mackerel are just as wonderful (photo, p. 75).

Per piece: about
- 35 calories
- 1 g fat
- 1 g protein
- 5 g carbohydrate

Red Pepper Cheese Bites

2	sweet red peppers, roasted	2
1 tbsp	olive oil	15 mL
1/2 tsp	crushed black peppercorns	2 mL
3 oz	mozzarella or Asiago cheese, cut in 1/2-inch (1 cm) cubes	90 g

● Cut peppers lengthwise into 1/2-inch (1 cm) wide strips. Toss with oil and pepper.

● Wrap 1 pepper strip around each cheese cube; secure with toothpick. *(Bites can be covered and refrigerated for up to 8 hours.)* Makes 24 pieces.

The mellow mozzarella and smoky roasted pepper make a unique flavor combo (photo, p. 75).

Per piece: about
- 19 calories
- 2 g fat
- 1 g protein
- 1 g carbohydrate

ROASTED GARLIC

Whole fresh heads of fat garlic cloves, slowly roasted on the grill, caramelize and mellow into a great appetizer. Press out each clove and spread on grilled Italian or sourdough bread.

● Rub off papery outer layers of 4 whole heads garlic. Cut off about 1/4 inch (5 mm) from tips. Arrange in double thickness of heavy-duty foil. Drizzle with 2 tbsp (25 mL) olive oil; top with 4 sprigs fresh thyme or rosemary.

● Loosely wrap foil over garlic, sealing tightly. Cook on grill over low heat for about 1 hour (or roast in 400°F/200°C oven or toaster oven for 45 minutes) or until soft and tender. To serve, squeeze out pulp. Makes 4 to 6 servings.

TIP: If you like, smash the soft cloves and whisk into mayo to spread over pitas or tortillas before filling. Or stir smashed clove into a vinaigrette to toss with new potatoes or greens.

Shrimp and Chives on Cucumber ▶

Chive blossoms are just one of the pretty edible flower garnishes you can pick from your garden.

Per piece: about
- 24 calories
- 1 g protein
- 2 g fat
- 1 g carbohydrate

1	seedless cucumber	1
1/2 tsp	salt	2 mL
1	pkg (5 oz/142 g) herb cream cheese, softened	1
24	small cooked peeled shrimp	24
	Chive blossoms or chopped fresh chives	

● Draw tines of fork lengthwise along cucumber to score; cut into 1/4-inch (5 mm) thick slices. Scoop out small amount of pulp from center of each slice. Sprinkle slices with salt; drain on paper towel for 1 hour. Pat dry.

● Using piping bag fitted with 1/4-inch (5 mm) star tip, pipe or spoon about 1 tsp (5 mL) cheese mixture onto each cucumber slice. Top each with shrimp; garnish with chive blossoms. Makes 24 pieces.

Stuffed Cherry Tomatoes ▶

Use a small coffee spoon to stuff the tomatoes — or try a pastry bag with a star tip, as professional chefs do.

Per piece: about
- 24 calories
- 1 g protein
- 2 g fat
- 1 g carbohydrate

3/4 cup	ricotta or cream cheese	175 mL
1/3 cup	chopped fresh basil or parsley	75 mL
4 tsp	olive oil	20 mL
1	clove garlic, minced	1
1/4 tsp	salt	1 mL
Pinch	pepper	Pinch
24	cherry tomatoes	24

● In bowl, beat cheese by hand until creamy; beat in basil, oil, garlic, salt and pepper.

● Using sharp or serrated knife, make X in bottom of each tomato; with small spoon, scoop out pulp through X. Using piping bag fitted with 1/2-inch (1 cm) star tip, pipe or spoon cheese mixture into tomatoes. Makes 24 pieces.

Endive Spears ▶

If Belgian endive is not available, you can use the small inner leaves of romaine or radicchio.

Per piece: about
- 22 calories
- 1 g protein
- 2 g fat
- trace carbohydrate

1/4 cup	mayonnaise	50 mL
2 tbsp	sour cream	25 mL
24	Belgian endive leaves (about 2 heads)	24
24	cooked peeled shrimp	24
	Dill sprigs	

● In small bowl, combine mayonnaise with sour cream; spoon about 1/2 tsp (2 mL) onto each endive leaf. Top each with shrimp; garnish with dill sprig. Makes 24 pieces.

(In center) New Potatoes with Smoked Salmon (p. 73), Endive Spears. (On large plate, clockwise from bottom) pork satays, Stuffed Cherry Tomatoes, Shrimp and Chives on Cucumber, Red Pepper Cheese Bites (p. 73), Marinated Mussels (p. 84).

Sushi 101 ◄

2-1/4 cups	water	550 mL
2 cups	Japanese sushi rice, rinsed and drained	500 mL
1/3 cup	rice vinegar	75 mL
1/4 cup	granulated sugar	50 mL
2 tbsp	mirin (rice wine)	25 mL
2 tsp	salt	10 mL
4	sheets nori (pressed seaweed)	4
	FILLING	
10	dried shiitake mushrooms	10
1 tbsp	soy sauce	15 mL
1 tsp	granulated sugar	5 mL
1 tsp	wasabi powder	5 mL
1	pkg (7 oz/200 g) frozen flaked crabmeat, thawed (or 2 oz/50 g smoked salmon, cut in strips)	1
Quarter	English cucumber, cut in long 1/2-inch (1 cm) thick sticks	Quarter
Half	bunch watercress	Half
2 tsp	sesame seeds, toasted	10 mL

● In 8-cup (2 L) saucepan, cover and bring water and rice to boil; boil for 2 minutes. Reduce heat to low; cook for 15 minutes. Remove from heat; let stand, covered, for 15 minutes.

● Meanwhile, in small saucepan, bring vinegar, sugar, mirin and salt to boil, stirring just until sugar dissolves; let cool.

● Spread rice in large shallow dish. Sprinkle with half of the vinegar mixture; toss with fork until combined. Toss with remaining vinegar mixture. Cover with damp tea towel; refrigerate for 45 minutes or until cooled to room temperature.

● Meanwhile, toast nori sheets by quickly brushing over element on high heat 10 times per side; set aside.

● FILLING: Meanwhile, in small saucepan, soak mushrooms in 1/2 cup (125 mL) warm water for 30 minutes. Add soy sauce and sugar; simmer for 10 minutes or until no liquid remains. Discard stems; slice caps thinly. Combine wasabi with a few drops of water to form paste.

● Place rolling mat *(maki-su),* clean place mat or folded tea towel on work surface with shortest side closest; place nori sheet, shiny side down, on mat. With wet fingers, press one-quarter of the rice evenly over nori, leaving 1-inch (2.5 cm) border on far side uncovered.

● Dab thin line of wasabi over rice 1/2 inch (1 cm) from closest edge. Top with one-quarter each of the crab, then mushrooms. Arrange one-quarter of the cucumber in row beside mushrooms; top with one-quarter of the watercress. Sprinkle with 1/2 tsp (2 mL) sesame seeds.

● Holding filling in place with fingers, tightly roll mat over filling. Using mat as guide, continue to roll up firmly, jelly roll-style, squeezing to compress. With sharp wet knife, trim ends; cut roll into eight 1/2-inch (1 cm) thick slices. Repeat with remaining ingredients. Makes 32 pieces.

Roll right into the world of sushi with this step-by-step approach. Serve as an appetizer, or prepare sushi for a summer lunch or picnic.

Per piece: about
- 65 calories
- trace fat
- 3 g protein
- 13 g carbohydrate

TIPS

● Japanese ingredients, such as nori, mirin and wasabi, are available in Oriental food stores.

● Sushi rice should be served the day it is cooked.

● Serve with a small mound of Japanese pickled ginger, and soy sauce blended with wasabi horseradish for dipping.

Smoked Salmon Spirals

Keep a roll of this elegant appetizer handy in the freezer. By the time guests settle, the roll will be ready to slice and serve with a glass of wine.

Per piece: about
• 25 calories   • 1 g protein
• 2 g fat   • 1 g carbohydrate

8 oz	thinly sliced smoked salmon	250 g
1	pkg (8 oz/250 g) light cream cheese	1
1 tbsp	chopped fresh dill	15 mL
1 tbsp	capers	15 mL
1	English cucumber, sliced	1
	Red onion strips and dill sprigs	

● Arrange salmon on plastic wrap in 12- x 8-inch (30 x 20 cm) rectangle. Mix cheese with chopped dill; spread over salmon. Press capers into cheese in row along one long edge; starting at capers, roll up jelly-roll style.

● Wrap roll in plastic wrap, squeezing to form smooth cylinder; twist ends to seal. Freeze for at least 4 hours or until firm. *(Roll can be frozen for up to 1 month.)*

● To serve, thaw for 10 minutes; slice thinly and arrange on cucumber slices. Garnish with onion and dill. Let stand at room temperature for 10 minutes. Makes 60 pieces.

Feta-Stuffed Cherry Tomatoes

This is a pop-in-your-mouth kind of appetizer, and a great vegetarian contribution to a buffet (photo, p. 37).

Per piece: about
• 28 calories   • 1 g protein
• 2 g fat   • 1 g carbohydrate

32	cherry tomatoes	32
1/3 cup	sour cream	75 mL
4 oz	cream cheese, softened	125 g
1/2 cup	finely crumbled feta cheese	125 mL
1	green onion, finely chopped	1
1 tsp	lemon juice	5 mL
1/4 tsp	dried oregano	1 mL
30	parsley leaves	30

● Cut tops off 30 of the tomatoes; trim bottom of each slightly to level if necessary, being careful not to cut through to pulp. With small spoon, scoop out pulp; place tomatoes upside down on paper towel-lined plate. Cover loosely with plastic wrap; refrigerate to drain for at least 1 hour or for up to 24 hours.

● Finely chop remaining tomatoes; place in small bowl. Add sour cream, cream cheese, feta cheese, onion, lemon juice and oregano; mix well. *(Filling can be covered and refrigerated for up to 24 hours.)*

● Using piping bag fitted with large star tip, pipe filling into hollowed-out tomatoes. (Alternatively, spoon 1 tsp/5 mL into each.) Garnish with parsley. Makes 30 pieces.

Spicy Crabmeat on Endive

1 cup	flaked crabmeat	250 mL
1/3 cup	light mayonnaise	75 mL
2 tbsp	diced celery	25 mL
2 tbsp	chopped fresh coriander	25 mL
2 tbsp	diced water chestnuts	25 mL
1/2 tsp	ground cumin	2 mL
1/4 tsp	each ground coriander and ginger	1 mL
Pinch	each salt and pepper	Pinch
24	Belgian endive leaves (about 2 heads)	24
24	sprigs fresh coriander	24

● In bowl, mix together crabmeat, mayonnaise, celery, fresh coriander, water chestnuts, cumin, ground coriander, ginger, salt and pepper. *(Mixture can be covered and refrigerated for up to 8 hours.)*

● To serve, mound heaping spoonful onto base of each endive leaf; garnish with coriander sprig. Makes 24 pieces.

E*ndive is an inspired holder for savory dollops.*

Per piece: about
- 18 calories
- 1 g fat
- 1 g protein
- 1 g carbohydrate

Make-Ahead Antipasto

2 cups	chopped carrots	500 mL
1 cup	chopped sweet green pepper	250 mL
1 cup	cauliflower florets, cut in tiny pieces	250 mL
1 cup	quartered mushrooms	250 mL
1 cup	chopped sweet pickles	250 mL
1/2 cup	chopped celery	125 mL
1/2 cup	pitted black olives, sliced	125 mL
1/2 cup	pimiento-stuffed green olives, sliced	125 mL
1/2 cup	small white pickled onions	125 mL
1/2 cup	chopped marinated artichoke hearts	125 mL
1	can (7-1/2 oz/213 mL) tomato sauce	1
3/4 cup	ketchup	175 mL
3 tbsp	olive oil	50 mL
1	can (6-1/2 oz/184 g) solid white tuna	1

● In large saucepan, bring carrots, green pepper, cauliflower, mushrooms, pickles, celery, black and green olives, onions, artichoke hearts, tomato sauce, ketchup and olive oil to boil. Reduce heat, cover and simmer, stirring occasionally, for 20 to 30 minutes or until carrots are tender-crisp.

● Drain tuna and add to vegetable mixture; simmer for 5 minutes, letting tuna break up into small pieces. Transfer to serving-size airtight containers. *(Antipasto can be refrigerated for up to 2 days or frozen for up to 3 months.)* Makes about 7 cups (1.75 L).

V*ivid with tomatoes, carrots and black olives and crunchy with celery, this savory antipasto is delicious spooned onto crackers or crusty bread.*

Per tbsp: about
- 14 calories
- 1 g fat
- 1 g protein
- 2 g carbohydrate

Satays — and more

Bite-size morsels of pork, beef, chicken or seafood are a crowd-pleasing addition to any appetizer tray.

Grilled Satays ▶

Strips of tender pork are threaded onto skewers to sizzle and caramelize over the coals. Serve with the deliciously dippable peanut sauce flecked with fresh coriander and green onion.

Per piece: about
- 70 calories
- 5 g fat
- 5 g protein
- 2 g carbohydrate

1 lb	boneless pork loin roast	500 g
1	slice (1/2 inch/1 cm thick) gingerroot, finely chopped	1
4	cloves garlic, minced	4
1/4 cup	teriyaki sauce	50 mL
3 tbsp	vegetable oil	50 mL
2 tbsp	chopped fresh coriander	25 mL
2 tbsp	rice vinegar	25 mL
2 tsp	grated lemon rind	10 mL
1 tsp	lemon juice	5 mL
1/4 tsp	hot pepper sauce	1 mL
1 tbsp	hoisin sauce	15 mL
1 tbsp	sherry	15 mL
1/3 cup	smooth peanut butter	75 mL
1/4 cup	finely chopped green onion	50 mL

● Trim any fat from pork; cut into 1-inch (2.5 cm) thick slices. Cut across the grain into 1/4-inch (5 mm) thick strips. Place in glass baking dish.

● In bowl, whisk together ginger, garlic, teriyaki sauce, oil, coriander, vinegar, lemon rind and juice and hot pepper sauce.

● Transfer 1/3 cup (75 mL) to measuring cup; whisk in hoisin sauce and sherry. Pour over pork, stirring to coat. Cover and refrigerate, stirring occasionally, for at least 2 hours or for up to 4 hours.

● Meanwhile, whisk peanut butter, onion and 3 tbsp (50 mL) warm water into remaining sauce. *(Peanut sauce can be covered and set aside for up to 4 hours.)*

● Reserving marinade, thread 1 piece of pork onto each of 24 soaked 6-inch (15 cm) wooden skewers. Place on greased grill over medium-high heat or under broiler; close lid and cook, brushing with marinade and turning once, for 3 to 4 minutes or until browned and just a hint of pink remains inside. Serve with peanut sauce. Makes 24 pieces.

VARIATIONS

● Substitute 3/4-inch (2 cm) thick boneless skinless chicken breasts or sirloin tip steak for the pork; cut across the grain into 1/4-inch (5 mm) thick strips. Cook chicken for about 4 minutes or until no longer pink inside. Cook beef for 4 to 6 minutes or until browned yet still pink inside.

TIPS

● Soak wooden skewers in water for at least 30 minutes before using to prevent scorching.
● For main-course servings, thread 2 or 3 pieces of meat onto each of 12 long skewers, leaving 1 inch (2.5 cm) between pieces.

Thai Beef Skewers ▲

*F*or an extra boost of flavor
and moistness, serve these
cocktail-size skewers with
peanut dipping sauce.

Per piece: about
- 28 calories
- 1 g fat
- 3 g protein
- trace carbohydrate

1 lb	flank, round or sirloin steak	500 g
3 tbsp	chopped fresh coriander or parsley	50 mL
2 tbsp	dry sherry or lime juice	25 mL
1 tbsp	wine vinegar	15 mL
1 tbsp	fish sauce or hoisin sauce	15 mL
1 tbsp	each dark sesame oil and liquid honey	15 mL
1 tbsp	each soy sauce and minced gingerroot	15 mL
1	large clove garlic, minced	1
Pinch	hot pepper flakes	Pinch

● Trim fat from beef; slice beef across the grain into 1/4-inch (5 mm) thick strips.

● In bowl, combine coriander, sherry, vinegar, fish sauce, sesame oil, honey, soy sauce, ginger, garlic and hot pepper flakes; add beef, stirring to coat. Cover and refrigerate for at least 2 hours or for up to 8 hours.

● Thread beef strips onto soaked wooden skewers. Broil for 3 to 5 minutes or until browned. Makes 30 pieces.

Pork and Pepper Mini Kabobs

2 tbsp	soy sauce	25 mL
2 tbsp	hoisin sauce	25 mL
1 tbsp	liquid honey	15 mL
1 tbsp	minced gingerroot	15 mL
1 tbsp	sherry	15 mL
2 tsp	rice vinegar	10 mL
2	cloves garlic, minced	2
2	green onions, minced	2
1 tsp	sesame oil	5 mL
1/2 tsp	cornstarch	2 mL
2	pork tenderloins (each about 12 oz/375 g)	2
1	each sweet red and green pepper	1

● In small saucepan, combine soy sauce, hoisin sauce, honey, ginger, sherry, vinegar, garlic, onions and oil; bring to boil. Dissolve cornstarch in 1 tsp (5 mL) water; whisk into pan and boil, whisking, for about 1 minute or until slightly thickened. Let cool.

● Meanwhile, trim any fat from pork; cut into 1/2-inch (1 cm) thick slices. Place in shallow glass dish; pour marinade over top. Cover and refrigerate for at least 2 hours or for up to 24 hours.

● Meanwhile, seed, core and cut red and green peppers into 32 bite-size pieces. Thread 1 piece of red pepper onto 6-inch (15 cm) soaked wooden skewer, then pork, reserving marinade, then green pepper. Repeat to make 32 skewers.

● Place on foil-lined baking sheets; broil for 4 minutes. Brush with reserved marinade; turn and broil for 4 minutes longer or until just a hint of pink remains in pork. Makes 32 pieces.

The crunchiness and color of sweet peppers complement juicy, tender morsels of pork.

Per piece: about
• 34 calories • 5 g protein
• 1 g fat • 2 g carbohydrate

Grilled Salmon Waves

1/4 cup	soy sauce	50 mL
1/4 cup	liquid honey	50 mL
1 tbsp	rice vinegar	15 mL
1 tsp	minced gingerroot	5 mL
1	clove garlic, minced	1
Pinch	pepper	Pinch
1 lb	salmon fillet	500 g
1	lemon, cut in 12 wedges (optional)	1

● In bowl, whisk together soy sauce, honey, vinegar, ginger, garlic and pepper. Remove skin from salmon; slice lengthwise into 12 long strips. Thread each strip onto soaked short wooden skewer; place in shallow dish. Pour soy sauce mixture over skewers, turning to coat well. Let stand at room temperature for 30 minutes.

● Reserving marinade, thread 1 lemon wedge (if using) onto end of each skewer. Place on greased grill over medium-high heat; close lid and cook, brushing often with reserved marinade, for 4 minutes. Turn and cook for 3 to 4 minutes or until fish flakes easily when tested with fork. Makes 12 pieces.

Strips of salmon fillet threaded onto skewers just need a quick marinade for flavor, a kiss of heat and they're ready to serve, impress and satisfy (photo, p. 17).

Per piece: about
• 60 calories • 7 g protein
• 2 g fat • 3 g carbohydrate

TIP: To remove skin from fish, place fillet skin side down. Gently slip sharp knife under skin at one corner of fillet. Using free hand, pull skin from side to side while pressing against skin with flat edge of knife.

Shrimp with Sweet-and-Sour Sauce

Make-ahead poached and chilled shrimp can be dipped in this glossy gingery sauce, or substitute your favorite Asian dipping sauce.

Per piece: about
- 17 calories
- 2 g protein
- trace fat
- 1 g carbohydrate

3	slices gingerroot	3
Half	lime, cut in wedges	Half
1 tsp	black peppercorns	5 mL
1/2 tsp	sesame oil	2 mL
1 lb	large shrimp, peeled and deveined	500 g
	SWEET-AND-SOUR SAUCE	
1 tsp	sesame oil	5 mL
1 tsp	grated gingerroot	5 mL
2 tbsp	granulated sugar	25 mL
1 tbsp	rice vinegar	15 mL
2 tsp	soy sauce	10 mL
1 tsp	cornstarch	5 mL

● SWEET-AND-SOUR SAUCE: In saucepan, heat sesame oil over medium-low heat; cook ginger, stirring, for 1 minute. Whisk in 1/4 cup (50 mL) water, sugar, vinegar and soy sauce; bring to boil. Dissolve cornstarch in 1 tbsp (15 mL) water; whisk into pan and boil, whisking, for 1 minute or until glossy and thickened. Let cool slightly. *(Sauce can be covered and refrigerated for up to 1 day; bring to room temperature before serving.)*

● In shallow saucepan, bring 4 cups (1 L) water, ginger, lime, peppercorns and sesame oil to simmer over medium-high heat. Add shrimp; poach for 3 minutes or until pink. Drain well. *(Shrimp can be covered and refrigerated for up to 4 hours.)* Serve shrimp with sauce. Makes 30 pieces.

Skewered Thai Shrimp

Mini kabobs are irresistible party pick-ups.

Per piece: about
- 11 calories
- 1 g protein
- trace fat
- 1 g carbohydrate

1/2 tsp	grated lime rind	2 mL
3 tbsp	lime juice	50 mL
2 tbsp	chopped fresh coriander or parsley	25 mL
2 tbsp	soy sauce	25 mL
1 tbsp	Dijon mustard	15 mL
4 tsp	granulated sugar	20 mL
1/4 tsp	sesame oil	1 mL
24	large shrimp, cooked	24
1	each sweet red and yellow pepper, cubed	1

● In bowl, whisk together lime rind and juice, coriander, soy sauce, mustard, sugar and oil; add shrimp. Cover and refrigerate for at least 2 hours or for up to 4 hours.

● Thread 1 red pepper cube onto short wooden skewer, then 1 shrimp, then 1 yellow pepper cube. Repeat with remaining ingredients. Makes 24 pieces.

MARINATED MUSSELS

Coriander and lime juice make a delicious marinade for mussels (photo, p. 75).

● Scrub 24 mussels (about 1 lb/500 g), removing beards; discard any that do not close when tapped. In large saucepan, cover and cook mussels in 1/4 cup (50 mL) water over medium heat for about 4 minutes or until mussels open. Discard any that do not open. Remove mussels from shells, reserving half the shells for serving. Transfer mussels to shallow bowl.

● Combine 2 tbsp (25 mL) chopped fresh coriander or parsley, 2 tbsp (25 mL) olive oil, 2 tsp (10 mL) lime juice and 1/4 tsp (1 mL) each pepper and hot pepper sauce; pour over mussels. Cover and refrigerate for up to 30 minutes. Arrange shells on serving platter; place 1 mussel on each shell. Garnish with 1 tbsp (15 mL) chopped sweet red pepper. Makes about 24 pieces.

Per piece: about • 15 calories • 1 g protein • 1 g fat • trace carbohydrate

Ginger Jalapeño Shrimp ▲

2 lb	large shrimp	1 kg
1/4 cup	vegetable oil	50 mL
1/4 cup	lime juice	50 mL
2 tbsp	minced gingerroot	25 mL
2	cloves garlic, minced	2
2	small jalapeño peppers, coarsely chopped	2
Pinch	pepper	Pinch
	Lime wedges	

● Peel and devein shrimp, leaving tails on; place in bowl. In blender, purée half of the oil, the lime juice, ginger, garlic, jalapeño peppers and pepper; pour over shrimp and toss gently to coat well. Cover and refrigerate for 1 hour.

● Discarding marinade, thread 3 or 4 shrimp onto each of 24 soaked wooden skewers. Brush 1 side of shrimp with some of the remaining oil. Place, oiled side down, on greased grill over medium heat or under broiler; close lid and cook, turning once and brushing with remaining oil, for about 2 minutes per side or until pink and firm to the touch. Transfer to serving plate; garnish with lime. Makes about 24 pieces.

Grilled over the coals in the summer or broiled indoors in the winter, these fuss-free seafood skewers are always a hit. The recipe works just as well with scallops or chunks of boneless salmon or halibut.

Per piece: about
- 41 calories
- 2 g fat
- 6 g protein
- 1 g carbohydrate

Cod and Potato Cakes (left) and Marinated Olives, Mushrooms and Onions (p. 87)

Cod and Potato Cakes ▲

Salt cod, soaked overnight before cooking, makes a tasty appetizer when shaped into little cakes and served with a mustardy sour cream sauce. This recipe can be doubled.

Per piece: about
- 66 calories
- 3 g fat
- 5 g protein
- 4 g carbohydrate

1 cup	mashed potatoes	250 mL
3/4 cup	flaked cooked salt cod (see TIP)	175 mL
2 tbsp	chopped green onion	25 mL
1/2 tsp	grated lemon rind	2 mL
1 tbsp	lemon juice	15 mL
1	egg	1
	Pepper	
	Vegetable oil	
	SAUCE	
1/2 cup	sour cream	125 mL
2 tbsp	chopped fresh parsley	25 mL
1 tbsp	white wine vinegar	15 mL
2 tsp	Dijon mustard	10 mL

● In bowl, mix together potatoes, cod, onion, lemon rind and juice, egg, and pepper to taste. Cover and refrigerate for 20 minutes or until firm enough to shape.

● Shape into twelve 1/2-inch (1 cm) thick patties; brush with oil. In nonstick skillet, cook patties over medium heat, in batches if necessary, for 3 minutes on each side or until browned and heated through.

● SAUCE: Meanwhile, mix together sour cream, parsley, vinegar and mustard. Serve with cod cakes. Makes 12 pieces.

TIP: To cook salt cod, cover with cold water; let soak for 24 hours, changing water several times. Drain off water. Cover cod with fresh cold water; bring just to boil. Reduce heat and simmer for 10 to 15 minutes or until tender. (Do not boil.)

Maritime Crab Cakes

2	pkg (each 7 oz/200 g) frozen crabmeat, thawed	2
1/2 cup	light mayonnaise	125 mL
1/4 cup	minced green onions	50 mL
1 tbsp	chopped fresh coriander	15 mL
1 tbsp	lime juice	15 mL
2 tsp	minced gingerroot	10 mL
1/4 tsp	hot pepper sauce	1 mL
1/4 tsp	each salt and pepper	1 mL
3/4 cup	dry bread crumbs	175 mL
2	eggs, lightly beaten	2
1/4 cup	vegetable oil	50 mL

● Drain and flake crabmeat; place in bowl. Add mayonnaise, onions, coriander, lime juice, ginger, hot pepper sauce, salt and pepper; mix well. Shape into 12 patties. Place bread crumbs in shallow dish. Dip patties into eggs, then into bread crumbs to coat all over.

● In skillet, heat 2 tbsp (25 mL) of the oil over medium heat; cook crab cakes, in two batches and adding remaining oil as needed, for 2 minutes per side or until golden. Makes 12 pieces.

Crab cakes are always the first appetizer to disappear off a party tray (photo, p. 17).

Per piece: about
- 125 calories
- 9 g fat
- 8 g protein
- 3 g carbohydrate

Honey Garlic Chicken Wings

2 lb	chicken wings	1 kg
1/4 cup	soy sauce	50 mL
1/4 cup	hoisin sauce	50 mL
1/4 cup	liquid honey	50 mL
2 tbsp	dry sherry or chicken stock	25 mL
2 tbsp	plum sauce	25 mL
1 tbsp	cider vinegar	15 mL
1	large clove garlic, minced	1

● Cut off wing tips; reserve for stock. Separate wings at joint; place in large shallow baking dish.

● Whisk together soy sauce, hoisin sauce, honey, sherry, plum sauce, vinegar and garlic; pour over wings. Cover and refrigerate for at least 4 hours or for up to 8 hours.

● Arrange wings in single layer on rimmed foil-lined baking sheet; brush with half of the marinade. Bake in 400°F (200°C) oven for 25 minutes. Turn wings over; brush with remaining marinade. Bake for 20 to 25 minutes longer or until juices run clear when chicken is pierced. Makes about 40 pieces.

Please company with a platter of properly sticky and burnished chicken wings.

Per piece: about
- 39 calories
- 2 g fat
- 3 g protein
- 2 g carbohydrate

MARINATED OLIVES, MUSHROOMS AND ONIONS

Round out any table of appetizer bites with a bowlful of this colorful olive and mushroom medley (photo, p.86).

● In skillet, heat 1/4 cup (50 mL) olive oil over medium heat; cook 2 sliced large red onions, stirring often, for about 5 minutes or until softened but not browned. Remove from heat. Add 1 can (14 oz/398 mL) pitted black olives, 1-1/2 cups (375 mL) whole button mushrooms, 1 tbsp (15 mL) balsamic or red wine vinegar, 2 tsp (10 mL) chopped fresh oregano (or 1/2 tsp/2 mL dried), and 1/2 tsp (2 mL) fennel seeds (optional); season with pepper to taste.

● Transfer to nonmetallic container; cover and refrigerate, stirring occasionally, for at least 4 hours or for up to 4 days. Makes about 4 cups (1 L).

Asian Meatballs

Styles change, but tangy hoisin-drenched meatballs are always a guaranteed crowd-pleaser.

Per piece: about
• 44 calories   • 4 g protein
• 2 g fat   • 2 g carbohydrate

1/3 cup	ketchup	75 mL
2 tbsp	hoisin sauce	25 mL
2 tsp	lemon juice	10 mL
1/4 tsp	granulated sugar	1 mL
1	egg	1
1-1/2 lb	lean ground beef	750 g
1/2 cup	minced green onions	125 mL
1/4 cup	dry bread crumbs	50 mL
2	cloves garlic, minced	2
1 tbsp	minced gingerroot	15 mL
1/2 tsp	dry mustard	2 mL
1/2 tsp	salt	2 mL
1/4 tsp	pepper	1 mL

● In bowl, whisk together ketchup, hoisin sauce, lemon juice and sugar; set aside.

● In large bowl, beat egg; mix in beef, onions, bread crumbs, garlic, ginger, mustard, salt, pepper and 1 tbsp (15 mL) of the ketchup mixture. Shape heaping tablespoonfuls (15 mL) into balls. *(Meatballs can be prepared to this point, covered and refrigerated for up to 24 hours.)*

● Place meatballs about 1 inch (2.5 cm) apart on rimmed baking sheet; bake in 400°F (200°C) oven for 20 to 25 minutes or until no longer pink inside, turning halfway through. Let cool for 2 minutes; toss gently with remaining ketchup mixture. Makes 36 pieces.

Cranberry-Glazed Meatballs

The sweet-and-sour flavor of cranberry sauce supplies a new dimension to meatballs and provides a change from the old familiar barbecue sauce. Don't forget the toothpicks so guests can skewer the meatballs.

Per piece: about
• 50 calories   • 3 g protein
• 2 g fat   • 5 g carbohydrate

1 cup	cranberry sauce	250 mL
1/4 cup	apple or orange juice	50 mL
1/4 cup	cider vinegar or red wine vinegar	50 mL
2 tbsp	packed brown sugar	25 mL
2 tsp	Dijon mustard	10 mL
	MEATBALLS	
1	egg	1
1 lb	ground chicken, turkey or lean beef	500 g
1/2 cup	fresh bread crumbs	125 mL
1/2 tsp	dried thyme	2 mL
1/4 tsp	each salt and pepper	1 mL

● MEATBALLS: In bowl, beat egg; mix in chicken, bread crumbs, thyme, salt and pepper until combined. Shape into 1-inch (2.5 cm) balls. Arrange in single layer in shallow baking dish; bake in 350°F (180°C) oven for 25 minutes or until no longer pink inside.

● Meanwhile, in saucepan, combine cranberry sauce, apple juice, vinegar, sugar and mustard; cook over medium heat, stirring occasionally, for 10 to 15 minutes or until thickened. Add meatballs; simmer for 5 minutes or until well coated. Serve hot. Makes about 32 pieces.

Roasted Carpaccio ▲

2 lb	rib eye or sirloin roast	1 kg
2 tbsp	olive oil	25 mL
4	cloves garlic, minced	4
1 tbsp	coarse pepper	15 mL
1 tbsp	chopped fresh rosemary	15 mL
1-1/2 cups	thinly sliced mushrooms	375 mL
4 oz	Parmesan cheese (preferably Parmigiano Reggiano)	125 g
3 tbsp	balsamic vinegar	50 mL
3 tbsp	extra virgin olive oil	50 mL
3 tbsp	chopped fresh parsley	50 mL
1/2 tsp	each salt and pepper	2 mL

● Trim fat from roast. Rub with olive oil, garlic, pepper and rosemary. Place in glass dish; cover and marinate for 30 minutes at room temperature or for up to 12 hours in refrigerator.

● Place roast in roasting pan; roast in 450°F (230°C) oven for 30 minutes. Let stand at room temperature, uncovered, for at least 30 minutes or until cool enough to easily slice as thinly as possible, trimming any fat.

● Arrange beef over large flat serving bowl; scatter mushrooms over top. With sharp knife, shave cheese as thinly as possible; scatter over mushrooms. Drizzle with vinegar and oil. Sprinkle with parsley, salt and pepper. Makes 10 to 12 servings.

Carpaccio is a popular traditional Italian dish prepared with raw meat. This cooked variation from food writer Bonnie Stern provides a perfect marriage of flavors for a delicious alternative.

Per each of 12 servings: about
- 195 calories
- 12 g fat
- 18 g protein
- 2 g carbohydrate

The Contributors

For your easy reference, we have included an alphabetical listing of recipes by contributor.

Jill Armstrong
Huron County Cheese Log, 37

Julian Armstrong
Chilled Vegetable Terrine with Parsley Sauce, 27

Elizabeth Baird
Blue Cheese and Walnut Spread, 46
Garlic Cheese Toasts, 10
Marinated Herring and Apple Spread, 47
Roasted Asparagus, 11

Donna Bartolini
Beggar's Purses, 69
Coconut Curried Chicken Phyllo Rolls, 69
Flaky Phyllo Cups, 56
Mushroom Crescents, 56
Phyllo Triangles and Fillings, 68
Roast Beef and Horseradish Phyllo Cups, 58
Savory Cheddar Thumbprint Cookies, 60
Smoked Salmon Eclairs, 61
Thai Crab Salad Phyllo Cups, 57

Laura Bickle
Feta-Stuffed Cherry Tomatoes, 78

Pam Collacott
Chèvre and Roasted Pepper Bruschetta, 13
Make-Ahead Antipasto, 79
Onion Cheese Bites, 6
Shrimp Croustades, 13
Smoked Salmon Cornucopias, 6

Ellen Cornwall
Herbed Crab Quickie, 42

Allison Cumming
Banana Curry Dip, 41
Leek and Brie Pizza Fingers, 10
Savory Phyllo Cups, 58

Nancy Enright
Herbed Cheese Ball, 34

Heather Epp
Smoked Salmon Spirals, 78

Carol Ferguson
Feta and Ricotta Spread, 46

Margaret Fraser
Brie with Cranberry Chutney, 31
Cod and Potato Cakes, 86
Egg and Watercress Sandwiches, 18
Marinated Olives, Mushrooms and Onions, 87
Poppy Seed Cheese Roll, 30

Kate Gammal
Hazelnut and Blue Cheese Tartlets, 55

Anne Lindsay
Barbecued Salmon Spread, 45
Fresh Beet and Onion Dip, 43
Thai Beef Skewers, 82

Jan Main
Jalapeño Stars, 59
Savory Cheddar Cheesecake, 33

Dana McCauley
Mushroom and Leek Pâté, 26

Rose Murray
Asparagus Cheese Toast Cups, 15
Black Olive Mini Pita Pockets, 19
Brandied Apricot Cheese Rounds, 47
Brie Walnut Toast Cups, 14
Dilled Shrimp Toast Cups, 15
Garlic Cheese Toasts, 10
Ginger Jalapeño Shrimp, 85
Goat Cheese and Sun-Dried Tomato Rounds, 47
Ham and Cheese Squares, 52
Mini Beef-and-Cress Sandwiches, 18
Pesto Spirals, 65
Roasted Asparagus, 11
Skewered Thai Shrimp, 84

Smoked Salmon Horseradish Butter Rounds, 47
Smoked Turkey and Chutney Sandwiches, 18
Versatile Toast Cups, 15

Donna Paris
Crostini con Funghi, 12

Daphna Rabinovitch
Turkey Sweet Potato Scone Sandwiches, 23

Iris Raven
Rice-Paper Spring Rolls, 65

Lucie Richard
Curried Cheesecake Pie, 34

Linda Stephen
Cranberry-Glazed Meatballs, 88
Rosemary Parmesan Shortbread Bites, 59

Bonnie Stern
Double-Salmon Terrine, 29
Gorgonzola Pâté, 37
Guacamole Pâté with Salsa, 28
Provençale Tuna Spread, 46
Roast Beef and Olive Rolls, 64
Roasted Carpaccio, 89
Smoked Salmon Pâté, 29

Lucy Waverman
Asparagus Strudel, 72

Canadian Living Test Kitchen
Almond Cheeseballs, 36
Artichoke Dip in a Snap, 43
Asian Meatballs, 88
Asian Veggie Dip, 40
Bite-Size Curried Shrimp Tarts, 50
Blockbuster Burger Bites, 19
Brie and Pecan Tartlets, 54
Caesar Tofu Dip, 44
Carrot Salad Bites, 17
Cheesy Crostini, 21
Christmas Quiche Wedges, 53
Classy Crêpe Cones, 62
Creamy Cheese Pear Pouches, 72
Creamy Chèvre Dip, 44

Photography Credits

LAURA ARSIE: cover
photograph of Elizabeth Baird;
photograph of the Canadian
Living Test Kitchen staff.

FRED BIRD: pages 14, 17,
25, 28, 39, 41, 53, 66, 70, 75,
76, 82.

DOUGLAS BRADSHAW:
page 81.

CHRISTOPHER CAMPBELL:
page 62.

YVONNE DUIVENVOORDEN:
page 11.

MICHAEL MAHOVLICH:
pages 4, 31, 85.

VINCENT NOGUCHI:
page 9.

JOY VON TIEDEMANN:
page 37.

MICHAEL VISSER: page 45.

MICHAEL WARING: page 42.

ROBERT WIGINGTON: front
cover; pages 7, 12, 19, 20, 23,
27, 32, 35, 49, 50, 51, 57, 59,
60, 69, 86, 89.

In the Canadian Living Test Kitchen. Clockwise from left: Elizabeth Baird (food director), Heather Howe (manager), Susan Van Hezewijk, Emily Richards, Donna Bartolini (associate food director), Daphna Rabinovitch (associate food director) and Jennifer MacKenzie.

Special Thanks

Praise and thanks go to the talented and enthusiastic team who put together *Canadian Living's Best Appetizers Made Easy.* First, to the Canadian Living Test Kitchen staff — home economists Emily Richards, Susan Van Hezewijk, Jennifer MacKenzie and manager Heather Howe — and to associate food directors Daphna Rabinovitch and Donna Bartolini for their leadership role in testing and creating recipes to appear in *Canadian Living* and in all of the cookbooks. Appreciation goes also to our valued food writers (noted above), managing editor Susan Antonacci, editorial assistant Olga Goncalves, senior editor Julia Armstrong, our copy department under Michael Killingsworth and our art department guided by Cate Cochran. Special thanks to our meticulous senior food editor, Beverley Renahan, for her high standards of consistency and accuracy and to editor-in-chief Bonnie Cowan and publisher Caren King for their support.

There are others to thank, too. On the visual side — our photographers (noted above); prop stylists Maggi Jones, Janet Walkinshaw, Shelly Tauber, Bridget Sargeant and Susan Doherty-Hannaford who provide the backgrounds, dishes and embellishments for the luscious food photos; and food stylists Kate Bush,

Ruth Gangbar, Debby Charendoff Moses, Lucie Richard, Olga Truchan, Jennifer McLagan, Jill Snider, Sharon Dale and Kathy Robertson who do the creative cooking, arranging and garnishing of recipes.

Book designers Gord Sibley and Dale Vokey are responsible for the splendid new design of the *Best* Series. Thanks also to Albert Cummings, president of Madison Press Books.

Working with Wanda Nowakowska, associate editorial director at Madison, is always a pleasure — certainly for her high standard of workmanship and creativity that have made the whole *Best* series so user-friendly and attractive, but also for her calm and always thoughtful, kind and generous nature. Thanks also to Tina Gaudino, Donna Chong, Rosemary Hillary and others at Madison Press Books.

Appreciation for their contribution at Random House is extended to Duncan Shields (mass marketing sales manager), Mary Jane Boreham, members of the marketing and publicity departments — Kathleen Bain, Pat Cairns, Sheila Kay, Cathy Paine, Maria Medeiros and Deborah Bjorgan — and president and publisher David Kent.

Elizabeth Baird

Index

Over 100 tasty nibbles for every entertaining occasion

CANADIAN LIVING
TESTED TILL PERFECT
KITCHEN

Trust Canadian Living to bring you the **BEST!**